The Path Has No Name

The Path Has No Name

✦

Life and Vision of a Sufi Teacher

Annette Kaiser

Edited by
Anna Platsch

iUniverse, Inc.
New York Lincoln Shanghai

The Path Has No Name
Life and Vision of a Sufi Teacher

iUniverse books may be ordered through booksellers or by contacting:

iUniverse
2021 Pine Lake Road, Suite 100
Lincoln, NE 68512
www.iuniverse.com
1-800-Authors (1-800-288-4677)

Translation:
Ellie Eich, Hawaii

Original Edition:
Der Weg hat keinen Namen
Leben und Vision einer Sufi-Lehrerin
Annette Kaiser, 2002 Theseus Verlag, Berlin
Die Theseus Verlag GmbH ist ein Unternehmen
der Verlagsgruppe Dornier

ISBN-13: 978-0-595-35023-0 (pbk)
ISBN-13: 978-0-595-79728-8 (ebk)
ISBN-10: 0-595-35023-2 (pbk)
ISBN-10: 0-595-79728-8 (ebk)

Printed in the United States of America

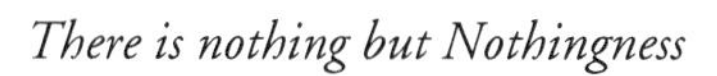

There is nothing but Nothingness

—Bhai Sahib

Contents

Foreword ix
Prologue 1
The Search 3
The Arena 20
The Sufi Color 24
The Path I 28
The Path II 38
The Love Affair 49
The Teacher 53
A Living Tradition 58
The Group 63
Ego Dissolution and the World of Appearance 67
Essence 73
Transmission of the Flame 77
Inquiry 80
Normal Human Being 89
Notes 97

Foreword

*I*n the summer of 2000, Annette Kaiser and I retreated to the tranquillity of a Greek island to carry on the conversations for this book. We stayed in a house on a bay with the name "Joyous East". It was precisely on the border between Orient and Occident; in the evenings we looked across at the lights of the Asia Minor coastline, a landscape full of the memories of not only Sufis but of the general history of humanity. We both had a deep feeling of an ancient belonging on this island.

Our intention was to make the path visible, which Irina Tweedie had shared with us—in its universality and in its vitality in addressing the unfolding needs and realities of the present day. To let the wide open spirit that blew through it become tangible.

Mrs. Tweedie was an educated woman—born in 1907 in Russia—who, after the chaos of flight and wars, lived in England, married, and worked for the Theosophical Society in London. Several years after the death of her husband, she travelled to India where she met, at the age of 54, the man who would be her teacher. Consciously, she had not been looking for him.

For more than five years she submitted to his hard and exacting teachings on the path of an Indian Sufi lineage.

In 1967, after her teacher had died and she had spent many months in the Himalayas, she returned to London and, in a small room above a loud intersection, began a meditation group with a very small number of people.

At the request of her teacher, she had kept a precise diary about her training, which first appeared in 1979 in a short form and then in 1986 in its entirety in English; in 1988 it appeared also in German and in many other languages.[1] Her group increased rapidly. She began to travel, within Europe, to the USA; she gave talks and seminars. But, she said again and again, we will never be many in number.

Her work changed, and her teaching began to distinguish itself from that of her teacher—not in essence but in form. She had truly carried the Path into the West and made it accessible to us. She died on August 23, 1999.

Annette Kaiser is one of two people who were authorized by Mrs. Tweedie to pass on the teachings of the Path. She lives in Switzerland and gives talks and seminars there and in Germany.

Only after we had returned from our conversations on the isle of Samos did we find out how much this island once had its place in a mystic culture at the source of *our* civilization, a culture in which the spiritual traditions of East and West were never separate; here, in the midst of our very own culture, was already the deep wisdom for which, today, so many people thirst.

We were amazed…

Chiemgau, February 2001
Anna Platsch

Prologue

***Mrs.** Tweedie never told us much about her personal history. Here and there a small anecdote, a detail from her childhood or the years in Vienna. She felt that her past was not important. The thing of most importance was in her book. You are ready to talk about your story now, Annette. What is it that brings you to take this step?*

I tell it simply because it could be helpful to other people. It's like a sample of a backward glance into the story of a person, to recognize the thread that represents the search. Everyone who looks back can, on reflection, find some similarity to the way the search had expressed itself earlier in his or her life.

I myself don't identify anymore with it. There is a sense inside where I feel that all of this has nothing to do with me as a person. We Sufis say that there's a certain point at which we discard personal history. This is not something that happens from outside. It simply falls away, because in the final analysis there is nothing else but THAT. No personal history. It is the world of appearance. It is relatively true. It is the wave on the surface of the ocean. And this is all only HIS mirror, a play in the world of appearance. It is important to express this. One leaves things behind. There is no past and no future, only the Present. And this is present in my innermost being.

The Search

Annette, how did you meet Mrs. Tweedie for the first time?

At that time I used to go to a book store in Bern, where I would just drift by the bookshelves and intuitively reach for this or that book. I saw *The Chasm of Fire,* took it in my hands, looked into it briefly, saw the picture of Mrs. Tweedie and said, "I have to read this."

I did read it, I think it was almost in one breath, and I just knew: "This is it. This is what I've always been searching for. This radical Path that goes to the root of roots, this is what I want. I have always looked for this." And with these thoughts burned the desire in my heart to come into contact with Mrs. Tweedie, as quickly as possible. At first I didn't even know whether she was still living or not. Then I got in touch with her through the publisher.

At this time I was involved with a group of people who were spiritually inclined and who were organizing the International Transpersonal Congress, which took place in Davos in 1983. I brought Mrs. Tweedie's book into this work-group. "This woman we have to invite. She is a great inspiration, a great teacher."

And so she was invited. And so, too, my first encounter with her took place. I had two small children at the time and although I helped somewhat to organize this Congress, it was not possible for me to be away for very long from my family. I really only had one day. I drove from Bern to Davos just to meet with Mrs. Tweedie. I had an appointment with her in the afternoon and was very stirred up. I knocked on the door of her hotel room. She opened to me, and from there on I don't know anything. I don't know what happened in this room. "Black-out" is not the right word for it, maybe—anyway, I can't say what happened.

That was my first encounter with her.

Towards evening a meeting took place with the Dalai Lama, who also took part in the Congress. Only a few people were invited to this reception. Among them was Mrs. Tweedie. There, for the first time, I consciously took stock of her: the older lady, her blue eyes, her deep blue eyes. More than that I can't actually say.

At that time you were working and had a family. How was your situation, actually?

Yes, at that time I was pretty tied down. My daughter was one and a half, my son was three and a half years old. I was married and we were both working. Because I really wanted to be there as mother for the two children, I stayed home half days. At the time I worked in quite a demanding job in a management position. I was with Swissaid, a private development organization that also helped women. In addition to this, I was learning t'ai chi. At the time I was already meditating regularly, which meant once or twice a day. For better or for worse, I took care of the vegetable garden in front of the house. My husband was better at that than I. I was responsible for the cooking and had the aspiration to bring body and mind together into some kind of balance. So it was a pretty intense day. That was my situation then. After the Congress in Davos came yet another duty. I was asked by the TAIS—the Transpersonal Association of Switzerland—which had organized this Congress, if I would take on the role as president, which I gladly accepted. So, I had one more task.

You were saying that at that point you were already meditating regularly. So you are saying that you were already consciously on a spiritual quest before you met Mrs. Tweedie. Can you talk about how that began for you in your life?

The search in all its facets definitely began early on. I grew up in quite a normal middle-class family. I had parents who were very engaged in their business and an older sister, one and a half years older than I, whom I loved more than anything. I grew up with baby-sitters who were just there to help us. I think until about the time I was 14, I lived like I was enveloped in a kind of bubble. Actually, I was barely confronted with the world. I lived pretty much in myself. That changed radically, though, when at 14 I went to Paris to work as an *au pair* girl in a convent. My sister had wanted to go to Paris to learn the language and I simply couldn't imagine life without her. So, I said, I want to go to Paris, too.

Even though you weren't yet finished with school?

Even though I wasn't yet finished with school. At the time I was in eighth grade. The convent was in the middle of Paris and belonged to a mission order—St. Joseph of Cluny was its name. There were seven of us girls from Switzerland who worked there. I had to do cleaning work and had to scrub the heavy casserole dishes in the evening. There I often went to church, more and more often. It wasn't that we were forced to go. I had been brought up Catholic at home, not strict. Although I went to church every Sunday, it was not dogmatic. We were relatively free.

And then, I still know exactly how it was, one Sunday the novices were singing at Mass. This singing touched my heart to such a degree that today I call it the *tauba.* It was HIS call that I became aware of. It was heart-rending for me. This song shook me to my depths. From then on I went to church every morning and wanted to become a nun. That was about one and a half months after I had arrived in Paris.

My parents had actually planned for me to take over their business. So I wrote to them relatively soon, after two or three months, to say that I wanted to enter the convent.

TAUBA

The Sufis differentiate between stages and mental states which the wanderer passes through and experiences. Today, the outer stages are no longer particularly emphasized. Nevertheless, one naturally does pass through them. *Tauba* is the first stage of the path, this is the beginning.

Originally the word meant "remorse". This is the moment when the soul turns, when one hears and heeds the inner call that leads back Home. The trigger can be an encounter, a sentence in a book, a leaf which falls from a tree, the moment of seeing a certain ray of light—*tauba* is unique for each person.

Other stages, for example, are *tawakkul,* perfect trust in God, surrender. This plays a significant role along the way. Closely connected to the process of surrender is *fana,* disappearing into God.

Individual stages are almost always broken down into yet others in classical Sufi literature—there are stages of patience (*sabr*), stages of gratitude (*shukr*), and stages of contentment (*rida*).

***How** did your parents react?*

Because they were Catholics themselves, they couldn't really say much against it. They probably thought, this is some kind of "tic" that will soon pass. They didn't say much. They didn't forbid it. My parents really showed a kind of greatness. They just let it be for the time being.

I myself was very shy and had learned at that time to observe myself quite precisely: which thought was with God and which thought was not with God.

***That's** pretty young to be having that kind of questioning going on. Did this come on your own or out of the context of the convent?*

It was just there. It wasn't that the nuns told me about it. It was just a very serious matter for me.

At that time I also got involved—in French—with reading about the saints. More than anybody, Therese of Lisieux really spoke to me. Her poems moved me deeply. I can still remember her poem "Flower Petals", how she entered into this ardent communion with Jesus, and how this was reflected in her poems.

> But the unpetalled rose is just flung out
> To blow away.
> An unpetalled rose gives itself unaffectedly
> To be no more
> Like it, with joy I abandon myself to you,
> Little Jesus.[1]
>
> *Therese of Lisieux*

She was a great inspiration for me. I let myself be guided by her and felt totally connected with her. She was also very young. I experienced an inner resonance. Basically, she just totally touched my life. Her influence is still with me, and a year ago I came across an article in which the lives of Therese of Lisieux and Al Hallaj were contrasted and their similarities elaborated upon. That was a real delight to see that I had perceived Therese of Lisieux to be a mystic long before I even knew there was such a thing.

I began to get into a lot of Christian women saints and at the same time scrutinized myself intensively, prayed constantly, said the rosary I don't know how many times a day...it was unbelievable! And at the same time cleaning, cleaning, cleaning. At that time, too, through the work I did at the home for the aged, I was confronted for the first time with death.

***Did** you talk with anyone about your inner experiences in the convent?*

Not at all.

So you were basically quite alone?

Yes, very alone, although the nuns were there. But interestingly enough, one didn't speak about one's inner life in this convent, and we girls hardly spoke among ourselves, either.

What also maybe threw a shadow across this period of time was the sharp separation beween worlds—here was the sacred interior world of the convent, and there, outside, was the wicked world. We sometimes had outings, too, to the Eiffel Tower or to a park. And there the view of the wicked world became more and more crystallized.

In the eyes of the nuns?

In the eyes of the nuns and how they talked about it. There was a kind of polarization with which I later had to struggle quite seriously in order to bring the two sides together. There was the interior life, this deep connection to God that was the essential thing, and then outside was this threatening world—the world of temptation, like it is understood in the Christian context. More and more this had developed as an attitude.

After a year I returned for a quick visit with my schoolmates, then I went to England for a year. Far away in Essex, to a former county manor with old people and four nuns. I was too young to enter a convent; I had to wait until I was sixteen. So this other community of nuns was recommended to me by the convent in Paris so that I could learn English for a year but still stay in a monastic atmosphere.

There were four of us Swiss girls; we were kind of locked in, as the estate was located far from any kind of civilization. We worked like dogs and were pretty exploited. I couldn't speak a word of English and was soon given the duty, along with cleaning, of attending to the sick people there. I had no idea how to go about it. For the first time in my life I saw a naked man and got quite a shock. I was told to care for three women who were no longer in their right minds. And this was at the age of fifteen, with no direction and no training.

I tried to pray. It was a time of great struggle. I really had the feeling that God had abandoned me. I prayed and prayed, and tried to feel in some way connected. It was very, very hard. And I didn't learn any English at all.

After six months, I packed my bags and told the nuns I was going on holiday. I knew that I wasn't coming back.

At first I approached an English family whom my parents knew. There I was able to stay for the time being. They found a new position for me, which was cleaning at a boarding school. But there I did learn English.

***But** didn't you write home? I'm surprised how many of these steps you managed by yourself, without your parents.*

I didn't want to tell my parents. I thought I should get through it myself. But my mother did notice something. She was very worried and came over to take me to this English family.

And something very decisive happened there. This family had three children—one son and two girls. And I was attracted to the son. Only in my mind, of course. That was it.

That year, at Pentecost, I was practicing the harmonium in a little chapel there. And suddenly the thought came to me that I could not have a true vocation if I could have such eyes for that young man. Because for me, at that time, a spiritual way and a worldly life were mutually exclusive.

I wrote to my parents that I would not enter the convent but that I'd come home and take over the business. I didn't know what else to do—I still needed some schooling and also wanted to go to a business school. My parents agreed. At the boarding school where I was working I had two hours of classes in the afternoons and the rest of the time I did cleaning. I was happy to be learning English but it was a tremendous challenge for me.

I cleaned the bedrooms and the toilets of girls my own age. I wiped their steps while they walked by. My father actually had enough money to send *me* to such a school, but by that time he probably thought that hard training makes for a strong person. It really got to me, to have to do this work. That was a hard lesson, a kind of life training.

At the end of the year I returned to my parents and attended the business school.

Although I noticed that I was an outsider at this school, I quickly became friends with someone who, so to speak, introduced me to the world. At the same time, I contacted my earlier piano teacher. I'd studied piano since I was seven. In those two years that I'd been away, something had happened to this piano teacher. She had become "a believer". I innocently began taking piano lessons again, which slowly turned out to be Bible study. She systematically pointed out to me that the Catholic Church didn't teach and live according to the Bible. And in many ways I had to say that she was right. So we had regular Bible study instead of piano lessons. I got to know the Bible inside and out, and severed my ties with Catholicism.

I also discovered at this time that I had many other possibilities in my life other than just taking over my parents' businesses. That was a very great disappointment to my parents and led to a deep estrangement between us. They told me they would pay for this school, and then I would have to fend for myself. They also didn't allow me to leave home before I was twenty. Legally, one was only then of age. So I had to live at home and that was a difficult time for me, as I was always under a certain kind of pressure.

I finished business school with the best grades, but as far as work was concerned, I had no self-confidence. I got a job as secretary in a bank. Inside, I was still very busy with my search for answers: what is God, what is the human being, what is the relationship between the two.

Along with work at the bank, I began to pursue my *Abitur* (equivalent to an AA degree from a community college) in evening classes. It was the time of the first communes, in 1968. I was fascinated with these people because they were intelligent, open-minded and bright. Nevertheless, I somehow felt quite different, as many people from this time will probably recall for themselves. I often had the feeling that I just could not go on, I couldn't make it. I was so deeply in despair that I didn't know anymore how I should go on living. There, at one point, my father helped me a lot. I spoke with him about how I was feeling and he understood.

So such trust was there that you could talk to him?

I always had an inner connection to my parents. I felt great love for my mother, and felt hers for me as well. Towards my father I would say it was more quiet. There was an inner level where we understood each other. But on the outside there was this breach. In any case, my father had the greatness to respect my free will. He also respected my decision not to follow in his foot-steps. Looking back, I am of course extremely grateful for what my parents made possible for me. In the situation at the time I didn't always see it like that. Today I feel respect for my parents and am grateful for the life that they gave to me. I also learned a lot from them.

A little while ago you expressed a deep feeling with which probably many who walk this path are familiar. This feeling of not fitting in, of not belonging, as though one were from some other world. When you look back now, is this actually a condition that is already a stage on our mystical path?

One is born that way. One is born a mystic. It's not like one wanted it, or was looking for it. It just happened. I see it really as a seed that blew into this life. And it develops, then, in its own way.

The only thing is, while one is in the phase of suffering, one doesn't know it yet. Our culture doesn't exactly value the inner mystical search anymore. The sense of a certain inability to handle life—that has something to do with this inner tendency, doesn't it?

Yes, that's true. But when one is in it, one doesn't see it, one just doesn't *know.*

For me, it also had to do with the spirit of the time. Those were the years of the 60's movement. Sexuality, for example, was unthinkable for me for a long time. I was too shy. On the one hand, it was my character; and on the other hand, it was the conditioning I had from the nuns in the convent and later from my piano teacher and all that Biblical hoopla.

And now I experienced day by day what was being lived, was also curious and wanted to find out things, understand the new thoughts. My mind wasn't at all closed to all the new ideas. I think that was another seed that was just given to me: I always wanted to know how and what this life is about. I always wanted to know what reality is. That was a deep urge that is still with me today—it just came with the package. Because of this I needed to come to grips with these new theories and ways of living.

Nevertheless, I, for myself, felt pretty inadequate. As I said, I had the best grades in school and then worked as the secretary for four staff trainers in a bank. That was a catastrophe. I didn't even know that white-out existed. I typed every letter five times and had absolutely no faith in my abilities. It was similar while I was finishing my *Abitur.* It was hell.

Next to this deep sense of inadequacy I felt an enormous tension in me between my intense religious search and the political movement, the interesting new ideas of the day. I didn't see any way to connect them. But I have to say that there was some inner help.

I slowly moved away from my piano teacher at this time because I felt her to be too dogmatic.

> Tell them they should not make absolute even a single piece of writing but to examine others, and also let them not think that they could tie my hands.[2]
>
> *Therese of Avila*

So, Catholicism wasn't it anymore, the Bible began to crumble, and I wanted to know, I wanted to get to the root. And so it came that I went to Israel, to the chosen people.

After the Abitur then?

No, that was still during the time I was going to evening classes. I think it was about in the middle of the last year of school. I was just 20, and I went to Israel with this girl-friend who introduced me "to life". I wanted to go to the Holy Land, I wanted to have a look at these people. I landed in Ramat Shalom, a year after the war between Israel and Egypt. Ramat Shalom was a small community of twelve people. Quite international. They were trying to build a village on the Golan Heights that would correspond with the mountain, the culture and the character of this region. I learned to shoot a machine gun, an Uzi. I can only say that I was lucky not to have come into any situation where I had to fight.

I learned to keep watch—every night I kept watch for two or three hours. The first time I stayed there for two weeks. And I met my first love. A man—his name was also George, like my present husband's—who was originally from Hungary, from the Warsaw ghetto, had survived Auschwitz, gone to America for an education and then come to Israel at the age of thirty to live there. Yes, and I fell in love with this man and wanted to marry him. And there I was confronted with Judaism. So I began to delve into the Jewish religion and anti-semitism because he wanted me to become Jewish.

We experienced a time on the Golan Heights that resembled on a small scale the way it was described in *Exodus*. Unbelievably intense. A walk along the edge between life and death, and in the middle was love. Later, on a second visit, during a rocket attack in Kiriaj Mona, we had a falling out. I realized that we came from two deeply different worlds and that truly sharing a life was just not possible.

It took a long time before I really got over him. One day I decided that I had to see him again. I started to look for him in a really strange way. I just asked every man or woman who looked Jewish if they had heard anything about George.

Whom you met in Switzerland?

Anywhere in the world. Very systematically, I asked if they knew this George. And one day someone knew him. I remember, I was in the train from Zurich to Bern and someone told me that he lived in such and such a place. Then I contacted him. He was married in the meantime and had two children. I met him after eighteen years. It was so beautiful. I met his wife too and knew then that a cup had passed me by.

I was deeply grateful for the experience but also infinitely glad that I had not married this man.

What did you do after you finished your Abitur?

I began to delve into science. I studied economics, but traveled around before that in South America. I went to Latin America, Central America, the USA, all by myself. I was alone on the road for six months. There I was again confronted with the world—in Guatemala with the Indians, with the guerrilla fighters—and I was so shocked about what was happening in the world that I told myself, I have to make sense of this, I just have to understand the connections. I didn't understand why people were killing each other in this way. So I began to study economics at the St. Gallen University. I dove into all the theoretical models of society and economy and noticed quite soon that they could not provide any answers to my questions. I was dissatisfied. I went to Berlin for awhile to study left-wing politics and philosophy in the hope that there I would find some answers. And partly I did get answers from Marx, Feuerbach, Hegel...answers that made sense to me. I also came into contact with the women's movement in Berlin. I returned to the University in St. Gallen and initiated the women's movement there. It was an extraordinarily creative time. Women made up only three percent of the population at the University then, but we brought the movement to the whole city. We opened up information stands, did theater performances, offered counseling to women, and in general tried to inform the public. If it didn't appear outwardly at that time, the questions were still going on inside of me—what is reality, what is truth? That was always the thread.

Where did you get the courage to try all that out, especially with your background? It really took a lot of courage to take on the traveling and everything else that you've mentioned.

Yes, I did have courage. That was actually never a problem for me. I wasn't afraid of traveling in the world, or of other civilitations. I loved everything far away, that had to do with native and simple cultures. I was deeply attracted to that. It was extraordinarily interesting to see how they lived, how they thought, what their culture and their perceptions were. This interest was just there in me.

The real difficulties were with my own experience. I was an emotional person, I lived from the inside out. But through my studies at the University, I learned for the first time to express myself. The intellectual training helped me to get along in the world. Suddenly I was able to present an argument, to classify and order and structure my thoughts. My education contributed to this greatly. That was a big change for me.

I have to add something else here. It was 1972 in Berlin. During this time I had looked into different life styles, checked out multiple relationships, same-sex relationship. I had tried out some of these things, looked into others and then come to the conclusion that it wasn't livable for me. Then there was this moment: I was standing in a bar around midnight. Until then the belief that God was guiding my life had been quite clear, in spite of historical materialism which denied all of that. But then came this inner voice that said, the thread is getting pretty thin. That was a turning point for me—the turning point in the attempt to find the Truth in science or in the theory of cognition. Because that had been my endeavor as I was studying Hegel, Feuerbach, Marx and the others. There was also Habermas, and later Wittgenstein. What is reality? I delved into these questions during my University years and at a certain point I had to see that Marx was also limited. I just wasn't satisfied with his explanations of reality. The use of natural resources and technological development were not exactly derived from Marxist theory, but these were urgent questions of the time. It was the same with the question of women—their role, their place in society, their reproductive role. I saw that Marx hadn't been able to cover this part of reality with his statement about historical materialism. This went hand in hand with my first "spiritual" book. At that time I was graduating. I had gotten the best grades, become a teacher's assistant and had received a national scholarship to work on my doctorate.

The theme of my dissertation was "Voices of the Feminine". My idea was to work on a model for an alternative to the nuclear family unit. That interested me. At the same time Ouspensky's first book came into my hands. It opened another dimension for me, one that was related to my search.

It was the time of experimentation, the whole wave of humanistic psychology began. Gestalt, primal scream, I don't know what all there was. I always observed it. I could not get into it, I was skeptical. I watched people and saw that even with all these therapies they essentially didn't change. Until one day, a woman in the cafeteria caught my eye. Waiting in the line at the cafeteria one could really see whether someone had changed or not. This woman caught my eye because suddenly she was able to wait. I watched her some more. And I noticed that she was behaving completely differently than she had a year before.

Something had happened to this woman. I talked with her and she said, "Yes, I've become a Buddhist. I go to the Tibetan monastery in Rikon; my teacher is there." She also told me that every Sunday evening there was a public talk given by Geshe Rabten. I thought, I'm going to go there. The woman has changed. That interests me. Then I went regularly to these talks. I saw that the Tibetans possess a knowledge about human beings. They talked about jealousy, envy, pride—all these properties that I knew in myself—and how to change these mental poisons into wisdom. I was fascinated, but I wasn't able to get past the outer appearances, the rituals. I just took in the talks and the presence of Geshe Rabten—that was enormous. He was like a mountain. He sat there—still, composed, serene. And that impressed me.

At the same time as this, pursuing my dissertation, I was trying to find ten exemplary women from the women's movement from the whole of Switzerland who had found an alternative lifestyle. I interviewed them and noticed quite soon that what I had defined as emancipated had just not happened for any of them. For me it was a frightening realization, a deep disappointment. I changed the theme of my dissertation and now my question was; "What prevents a person from living his life freely, both from the outside and the inside?" For the external question, I had all the models and concepts of society that I'd studied, but for the inner one I entered new territory. I took in aspects of psychology but that wasn't enough. I got acquainted with the teachings about karma and began to explore them for myself. I finished the dissertation and actually found many answers to my questions. I also knew that the dissertation would not be accepted as it was. But for me finding out the truth was important. I turned in the work and the professors said, "Yes, Ms. Kaiser, just change this and that, and you also have to take this out." And I said, "No, I can't do that. What is here has been investigated conscientiously and then written to the best of my knowledge."

Although by this time I'd taken all the prior exams needed to finish, I let it drop and told myself that one day I would get to a point that would represent something like my own doctorate. A couple of years ago I did dream that I received the degree of doctor.

I had come full circle.

***Was** the material that you were supposed to remove what we'd call "spiritual material" today? It was certainly not scientific, from the standpoint of your doctor-elders.*

That's right.

***How** did it go on from there?*

I got married and went from St. Gallen to Zurich for a year. Then I got pregnant, and as you know, pregnancy opens one to new spaces. For the first time, for example, I saw an angel. It was an impressive experience, as suddenly this other kind of being appeared.

We moved to Bern at the time of the birth. I finished writing my dissertation and began to read. I was looking. At first it was just books as there wasn't anything else accessible to me. But pretty soon after the birth of my child, I met a gypsy on the train between Zurich and Bern. She was so touched by this child sitting on my lap that she referred me to someone in Bern. I had told her that I had spiritual interests but that I couldn't go to Rikon anymore with a baby. She told me she knew a woman in Bern who taught yoga. So I went a few times to Siddha yoga and began to do this correspondence course with Swami Muktananda, which was based on Patanjali yoga. I did this course for seven years. Twice a month I received new material. That opened up for me another understanding of the world. It was very helpful to grow from the concept of historical materialism into a spiritual picture of the world.

Every step, each one of these parts of my life that I've talked about has a blessing hidden in it. For example, the knowledge I acquired about Marx and in the philosophical writings of Feuerbach and Engels allowed me to see the dangers of religion. How dogmatic, how fundamentalist it can be, truly an "opiate for the people". This helped me to examine things on an intellectual level, not to simply accept everything or to believe blindly, but first to check it out and then again to weigh it inwardly, to find out what I could see as true or relatively true—how I thought of it and felt it for myself. That helped me a lot.

Before my second child came into the world in 1981, I had three wishes to fulfill: to get to know Swami Muktananda, to go to the Esalen Institute, and to meet Evelyn Eaton. I had gotten her book *I Send a Voice* and been very moved by it. At the time, I wrote to her immediately and simply thanked her for this wonderful book.

As I planned my trip, I saw that she lived not far from my route, and I wrote and asked her if I could come and see her. I was eight months pregnant with my daughter at the time…

***Did** your husband and son come with you?*

No, I went alone.

***And** your husband stayed with your son?*

Yes, he made a lot of things possible for me, which wasn't always easy for him.

I landed in Bishop and was picked up by Edith, a helper of Evelyn Eaton, who was at the time already in her eighties and was ill. I was brought to her and she greeted me and that was all.

I slept there and every night I had dreams in which Indians played a central role. I more or less dreamed the story of the Paiute tribe. It was incredibly intense, but I didn't really know why I was there. I was there a whole week and I still didn't know. Edith brought me then to a few places, we did the pipe ceremony, she taught me the medicine wheel, and I still didn't know why I was there. In the book, Evelyn Eaton described how it took seven years until she received the pipe. And suddenly I knew I had to ask Evelyn Eaton for the pipe. I was taken to her right away and I asked her if I could have the pipe. Evelyn Eaton answered that I had fulfilled all the conditions, and said yes.

Then everything happened very fast because I only had two days left. I was supposed to go into a sweat lodge.

***Being** so pregnant? Weren't you afraid?*

No. But once I was inside I did get scared. It did get kind of weird for me somehow, but there were different reasons. Beforehand I wasn't afraid, I wasn't really concerned at all. I had to prepare different things. I was supposed to prepare a meal for the community, I had to sew some little pouches, and so on. Then I went into the sweat lodge. The teacher of Evelyn Eaton, a tribal chief named Raymond, who I later learned was a well-known shaman, worked there as caretaker of the sweat lodge and conducted the ceremony.

He carried it out quite gently as I was so advanced in my pregnancy. It was just very impressive. We prayed, sang and again prayed from the bottom of our hearts in this terrible heat and total darkness. In this blackness. In this way everything melted away, and in the end also the fear.

The pipe ceremony was on Sunday. Evelyn Eaton passed the pipe over to me, explained to me exactly how to do everything and told me it was a *working pipe*, I was to work with it. So, I took all these experiences home with me and for a long time did the pipe ritual for myself. To do it, one sits oneself down on the ground in nature, gets everything ready, begins to fill the pipe with tobacco all the while calling on all the directions, Wakan Taka—the Great Spirit—and Mother Earth. Praying, one lights the pipe and every pull is done with an inner prayer. A pipe can be smoked for different purposes—for example, as a contribution toward world peace, for a person who has a problem or is sick, or when one's own questions are there.

Did you know at that time what a working pipe is, what it means?

No, not yet at that time. I just smoked the pipe as I'd been instructed and learned a lot about nature as I went along. I learned to read the signs, like reading a language. I still do the pipe ceremony today and teach my daughter, so that the tradition is carried on. The pipe is a wonderful symbol. You have the mineral kingdom, the plant kingdom—the tobacco is actually the thing that is your ego, which gets burned up through the ceremony, and you just give your-self up completely. It is like meditation. You become empty. At the end there is nothing left—like in the pipe. Doing this, one prays in the different directions and offers respect towards the whole of creation and for Mother Earth, and prays for the benefit of all beings.

I did this at home and two years later—I couldn't go back because I had the children—I had a dream in which Evelyn Eaton died. She was a writer, by the way—her life was really interesting; for example, during the second world war, she was one of the first woman correspondents who went to Europe as a reporter. She had taught at different universities and then between the age of fifty and sixty lived in a stone hut with no water or electricity, totally secluded and solitary. Later she organized classical concerts with famous artists in the middle of the desert. She was a pioneer woman like Mrs. Tweedie—maybe not on the same level, but in any case a pioneer woman. I dreamed how she—how her soul—rose into the sky as a white feather. Then I knew that she had died. I told Mrs. Tweedie about her too. Mrs. Tweedie told me one time that she saw an Indian behind me. She told me a couple of times that she herself had memories of the shaman world.

Evelyn Eaton was my second station in America; the first was Esalen. There I learned t'ai chi. I had actually signed up for a course in shamanism, but after my 24 hour flight, I needed movement. There happened to be a t'ai chi seminar taught by Chungliang Al Huang. I came in and knew: this is it. On a certain level, movement had always interested me. I always did a lot of exercise and I did yoga with Mr. Yesudian. But I found the movement more dynamic in t'ai chi, and—different than in dance, for example—it had a deeper philosophical dimension. In yoga one had to lie down and one needed a mat, whereas I simply could do t'ai chi anywhere in the world. Because I was travelling around a lot doing aid work, it was ideal for me.

The third station was Swami Muktananda. I went to him and knew that he was not my teacher. So, I turned around and went back home, without a teacher.

During this time I came into contact with someone who was very involved in Tibetan Buddhism, especially with the Kagyu school. I started with the Ngondro practice, basic exercises among which prostrations is one, and practiced the Dorje Sempa meditation. I also received other initiations, for example the Powha initiation. This is a practice which helps get a person ready to die. It's a very powerful practice. I received the initiation at the time from Ayang Rimpoche. I practiced everything very diligently; I got up early every morning before the children woke up. It gave me energy for the whole day. In the afternoon I had a "Mama hour", when the kids had to leave me alone. Then I practiced again. And at the new moon and full moon there were other special meditations to do. It really helped me to purify my spirit, to compose myself. One works in this tradition also with visualizations, and I learned to see the world as a manifestation of Buddha lands and perceived people more as aspects of Buddha. This gave me the possibility to *truly* get along in this world, not just intellectually but also with my whole being...being anchored strongly in an inner world allowed me to see the outer world in its relativity. But I had no teacher. The Karmapa could have been a teacher for me, but he was no longer alive.

Somewhere inside of me I had a deep image of what and how a teacher should be. That was one thing. The other was, at that time, Tibetan Buddhism was a monastic way. I suffered unbelievably from this because I saw no possibility for me as a householder to experience enlightenment or to "come Home", as I just didn't have the necessary time for the practice. To become a Lama I would have had to retreat into a cave for three years, three months and three days. I did not have this possibility. But my longing to come Home was incredible.

That was the situation in which I happened upon Mrs. Tweedie's book. She became the Gateless Gate for me—a possibility to come Home *and* to have a family. Standing in the middle of life. It was an incredible deliverance to find this path. And in addition, I could go to see her. She wasn't like the Dalai Lama—one could have gone to him as well—but with two small children? I could not go to Dharamsala. Mrs. Tweedie was also not surrounded by a staff of monks which prevented one from entering into a personal relationship.

As President of the Transpersonal Association in Switzerland, I got to know a lot of teachers outside of their lectures. I have to say that only a few resonated with this inner picture I had of a teacher. Mrs. Tweedie did. She stood up to all of my scrupulous inspection. Later she would often tell us that one had to test a teacher precisely and by one's highest standards. Without knowing it, that's what I did.

After the emancipation movement in which one had renounced all authority, it had become clear to me how helpful a person could be who was more evolved than oneself. I didn't know who Mrs. Tweedie was. She only confused me. I could not classify her at all. I only watched her. I was only fascinated and pulled in. It was as if I was following a thread that she was pulling around herself—or maybe she wasn't pulling. I don't know. I continued to do my Tibetan practices. I think that for two or three years I just watched her.

The Arena

So*, this long search came to an end on the outside and you often went to London to see Mrs. Tweedy.*

Yes, and twice a year I got to invite her to Switzerland. That was always an intense encounter, an intensive time. I did not understand a thing in the talks. By that, I mean I was just gone. I didn't know afterwards what had happened. I had no idea about Sufism. It also didn't really interest me. That was not the question.

During this time I noticed that I was able to stabilize myself with Tibetan Buddhism. Something got quiet. With this Mrs. Tweedy, though, it was becoming clear that I was going to encounter my dark side. I was going to encounter myself. Slowly I realized this. I was incredibly fearful of this and would inwardly squirm, thinking, how does it feel to just do this Buddhist practice? It felt gray. Gray! On the other hand I had this incredible experience with Mrs. Tweedy. I knew that one day I would have to jump. That was in March. Mrs. Tweedy had a talk, she was ending a whole series of talks. I went to her and asked her if she would accept me as a disciple. And I gave her the most treasured thing I had. She only said, "Yes, you mean it seriously." And that was that.

This step had incredible consequences. I wanted to live truthfully.

I tried to be truthful in every aspect of my life. I examined each arena of my life and it almost came to an explosion. I gave up my chairmanship at the Transpersonal Association of Switzerland and stopped working as representative for my t'ai chi teacher. Instead, I followed my own inner picture of what I understood t'ai chi to be—to be at one in this life, to be in harmony, in wholeness.

I also ended my work with Swissaid and from then on only worked freelance in aid organisations.

Then there was—and this was devastating—the relationship issue with my husband. Over the years we had paid too little attention and so there, too, a breach happened. With that, actually all of the essential areas of my life were quite brutally broken. I stood in front of a great nothingness. In relation to the family, of course, it was a gradual process. It was very important for me not to create new karma. I did not want to hurt anyone, I wanted the best solution for all four of us: for my husband, my son, my daughter and for me. I was ready to stay in the family or to go. We both decided on separation. Although I had an inner vision of this, as though the family was expanding. I saw an inner picture, like an Indian tribe. Today, I think that it has become like this. Today I know that it was for the well-being of everybody.

You said that the first step after your "jump" was truthful examination of your life and that through that the structures had come undone. This means that there must have already been something there in your depths that opened up at that moment. So something happened which you had already been longing for. The question is, didn't it hurt anyway? Wasn't it painful that your family had fallen apart? That you gave up parts of your career? That you said good-bye to your t'ai chi teacher?

Yes, it was really like an explosion. An explosion in every part of my life. All the structures crumbled. It was an incredible disorientation that happened in me. It was deeply frightening. On the outside, I had no orientation anymore; I had only an interior one. But this was still unclear on a conscious level. I had many doubts about whether everything was right. I suffered terribly, especially because of my family. For me that was—I can hardly find words for it—the deepest pain. Very, very difficult to bear that, to bridge it, to somehow deal with it. But help would appear during the worst times, like for example this inner vision when I suddenly saw us all in this tribal relationship. There I got this sense of certainty that it was all right. I also could continue to go see Mrs. Tweedy. I also talked with her about it and received great support from her—not so directly, but simply from the fact that I could go there, that I was accepted. In all of these doings I felt that I was being carried. But it was an incredibly heavy time. A time of extreme uncertainty. On the outside I had lost everything. I didn't know how to go on.

And how did it go on?

First of all, I had set as a priority to go as often as possible to Mrs. Tweedie and to be present in myself. That gave me this inner feeling of being carried.

Maybe I should distinguish between an outer and an inner level. On the outer level, I was taking pains to fulfil my responsibilities towards the children in the best possible way.

My husband and I made the effort to separate peacefully. I put a lot of energy into creating the separation so that love stayed in our hearts. This demanded a lot of attention. During this time I also met George, my present husband. That was a support for me in the outer sphere as well.

On the outer level, it just took time, to endure and see it through, and somehow in the course of time everything came into more of a balance. I taught t'ai chi. This was my second source of income next to the freelance work I did with aid organizations. And now I taught it in my own way. I no longer worked within the organization of my teacher. I had my t'ai chi group and I continued with it fairly consistently. During this time in which I lived pretty quietly I also wrote my first t'ai chi book. In this way something was shaping itself in this empty space, something that could be carried out into the world. I began fairly soon to host a meditation group. I asked Mrs. Tweedie if that would be all right; so twice a week the meditation group took place.

You stopped doing the Buddhist practices at this time?

Yes, that was a clear break. I concentrated completely on this Sufi path. I let everything else be and practiced what was given to us, the Dhyana meditation. And relatively soon I received the mantra from Mrs. Tweedy as well. Those were the two things that I really tried to constantly practice.

Before we continue, I'd like to describe my first encounter with Mrs. Tweedy in London. She had invited me to come to London. I was returning from Africa where I had had an assignment in an aid program and I had a stop-over in London on my way back to Europe. I always tried to do this in the coming years as well, to have an interval in London on my way back.

So I arrived at her house for the first time, and she greeted me cheerfully, saying that first of all she had to clean the bathroom and the toilet. That there had been a hundred people here, that I needed to have a clean toilet. I was totally bewildered. I had imagined something quite different when one comes to visit a spiritual teacher. That was the first thing; the second thing was that she cooked a meal for me. It was lunch time. Spinach with fried eggs and potatoes. And inwardly I was waiting for a spiritual conversation to begin. But it was not like that. After lunch she said that I should sleep now, I should lie down, I must be dead tired. So I lay down. Occasionally, between spinach and tea, came a word or a sentence that made me listen attentively. But overall, I couldn't make sense of it.

That was my first encounter with Mrs. Tweedy in London. Without people being around her, without her functioning in her usual role. I slept at her house two nights and that has impressed me to this day. Only much later did I understand that there is nothing that is not spiritual. That everything belonging to life, the whole scale from cleaning the toilet to being immersed in absolute stillness is not separate. It made a deep impression on me.

Very soon after that I had a dream in which Mrs. Tweedy stood at the door and said to me: "I have been waiting for you" and a symbol was given to me. I believe think this was a kind of initiation dream.

The Sufi Color

Y*ou were saying that when you first met Mrs. Tweedy you were still following a Buddhist tradition. That was at a time when there was still very little Sufi literature around. You said that you went to see her after you had read the short version of her book and that during the first years you were only observing. Later you certainly read other literature about Sufis besides Mrs. Tweedie's book, although her book contains the whole Sufi tradition in essence. From your point of view today, what are the characteristics of Sufism?*

That is a big question. In answering that, I'd like to return once more to the beginning. When I met Mrs. Tweedy, I didn't know that she came from the Sufi tradition. I was just fascinated by this radical path, by this merciless/merciful way. I was fascinated by the fact that there is a way that brings people home—standing in the middle of life. My heart was deeply delighted to encounter this mystical path. To begin with, the name—the packaging—did not interest me. It took a long time for it to come in. And somehow that also has something to do with the tradition. Bhai Sahib—Mrs. Tweedie's teacher—says quite clearly that it is not a philosophy, not a religion—it is a way of life. That hits the nail on the head. Everyone remains or can remain whoever he or she is. A Christian, a Hindu, a Moslem—it doesn't matter. And in its essence this path is nameless. This is its innermost core. Bhai Sahib says that our path is as old as humankind itself. This is a central statement. It is about being human, becoming a conscious human being"? Beyond any kind of dogma or color, it's about this desire which has always existed that the human being—who is the only creature in the world with this possibility—might know himself and, with that, know God.

How we come to this realization is something else. This path contains thousands of years of experience. The ancient wisdom within it offers a way to self-realization, how to become one with THAT which cannot be named. From today's point of view, I would emphasize more the Nameless. To me, this has something inherently universal to it. Universal consciousness. One could also say interdenominational spirituality—religion in the sense of "religio"—connecting back to the root. Today it's no longer about emphasizing difference. There are different pathes, that is not the question—it's also good that there are differences. But the spotlight today is on what is common to all.

This path was given a name by other people. It is a pathless path, not simply a path. It is a pathless path that was given different names from the outside. One name was *safa*, another was *Kamal Posh;* the last name that was given this path was the *Sufi* path. *Suf* means wool, or also soft, soft as wool. That the path goes by the name "Sufism" has to do with a story the Sufis tell that the "wool-coat wearers"—our ancestors, as it were—traveled around seeking teachings from every great prophet, and finally received an understanding for the "Essence of the Essence" from Mohammed. Today, as "Sufis", they have moved beyond the form of conventional religion. Historically, the Sufis were often not well liked, as is true for many advocates of a mystical path, because they experienced God directly and this lies beyond any dogmas. This makes people free. It is a basic human experience that frequently runs counter to many institutional religions.

A Sufi is a person who is nobody, who is nothing. A Christian mystic is a person who is nothing. A real Hindu or Advaita is someone who is nothing. We share the essence of all mystical paths. What Mrs. Tweedie through Bhai Sahib and his teacher passed down to us is a lineage which contains the wisdom, the experience of being able to mirror people, to lead them to recognize their own inner teacher. This mystical path offers people a way to recognize their Higher Self, to recognize their Being. I think it is still a rarity to find a path that is able to show this so clearly to people.

Nevertheless, I see every mystical path as having equal value. Fortunately there are different ones. Today there are many more mystical paths accessible to human beings than thirty or forty years ago. That has to do with the evolutionary movement of humankind.

People are different, and based on the inner resonance there have to be different mystical paths. In essence, all mystical paths lead to the same place. A path is like a boat that brings the person to the other shore.

A wanderer sees a great flooded river ahead of him, the bank on the near side uncertain and dangerous, the other one safe and without danger. But there is no ship to cross nor is there any bridge to the other shore. He thinks: perhaps I could gather reeds and tree trunks, sticks and leaves, build myself a raft from these things and, working with hands and feet, reach the other shore unharmed. He carries out this plan and reaches the other shore unharmed.

> Having reached there, he thinks: this raft has been of great use to me; I will load it onto my head and shoulders and take it with me wherever I go.
>
> But how would he act correctly? He would think: although this raft has been of great use to me, nevertheless I will set it down on dry land or sink it in the water and unencumbered I will go wherever I want. If you understand the parable of the raft, then give up (when you have reached the goal) even the true doctrine, and still more the untrue ones.[1]

In the end one has to leave the boat behind and the pathless path actually does become pathless. I think that our path, our Sufi path of the Naqshbandiyya-Mujaddidiyya—this is an Indian Naqshbandi lineage—has certain characteristics that resonate with certain people, with their inner alchemy. The pillars of our pathless path are the Dhyana meditation and the practice of saying the mantra, the *dhikr.* These are the actual pillars that carry it. In addition to this, there is the dream work.

Dhikr

> *Dhikr* is an important practice in all of the Sufi lineages. In the Naqsgbandi tradition it is done in silence. It is similar to what we know as saying mantra or *Japa* practice from the Indian traditions—it is the constant repetition of a divine name or attribute, or of a divine declaration.
>
> *Dhikr* comes from Arabic and means to remember, to recollect, to call.
>
> At the beginning, the disciple practices *dhikr* consciously and with effort. "And if we forget to say the mantra," Mrs. Tweedie often said, "then we don't criticize ourselves about it. We see it and we again begin anew."
>
> Layer by layer the *dhikr* penetrates into the inner levels of the heart, which slowly open in the process. Later the *dhikr* "happens", and often eludes conscious perception.
>
> It is important for the transforming power of the *dhikr* that it be passed on by a living master, even though today we no longer have visible initiations.
>
> In this lineage, we work with the mantra *Allah*, the naming of the Divine without attribute, signifying emptiness in its ultimate meaning. No language is so near to the heart like Arabic, say the old Sufis. A breath (the h) remains at the end of the mantra and refers to the Divine concealed in the breath. In this way the *dhikr* also becomes united with the breath: *al* with the outbreath, *lah* with the inbreath. After practicing awhile, the breath too carries the Divine naming in silence.

"Every breath which is taken without remembering God is squandered," say the Sufis.

Dhikr leads us deeper and deeper into a kind of polishing of the heart. It is the aspect of remembering our being before we were.

"The reality is the *Jap*. The longing. The faith. The sweetness of resting in Him in deepest peace."[2]

The Path I

What did you know at that time about the path as you came to see Mrs. Tweedie?

Actually very little. I just practiced the Dyhana meditation and the mantra. I went as often as I could to Mrs. Tweedie, as often as it was possible with my duties and my family. For me, it was about her presence. I didn't understand intellectually what was happening there. I just went. Dreams were related, questions were asked and tea was drunk in the group that sat in her living room. At the beginning, when every weekday was still open and everyone could still come, it was really crowded. It was not exactly fun to be there. We sat in the most uncomfortable way with our legs pulled in because it was so full of people. It was hot in the summer. It was also hot in the winter in this crowd of people. I very soon got to know the nature of projection—how one can get all upset over individuals in the group, how these people can disturb one, how maybe one can get jealous of those who always were able to sit at Mrs. Tweedie's feet or of those who rushed into her house first. All of these human things. And I understood very soon that these were also *my* issues and, based on what was going on there, tried to withdraw the projections and take a look at things. Slowly, in this way, I got to know my shadow sides, my dark sides, my split off sides. Added to that was the dream work. I began to really look at my dreams and in the course of time learned that I was not at all who I thought I was. I gradually learned that the whole world is contained in a person, not the other way around—that the person is in the world. These are the initial processes. At the beginning I had a phase with Mrs. Tweedie where I was very unencumbered. I told her everything, really everything. That was such a deliverance for me. The most secret things, the most impossible things. I travelled around a lot in the world and experienced quite a bit. She always had an open heart, an open ear for everything. She never judged anything.

I could talk to her about everything. That was an enormous opportunity for me. She was someone who had a deep understanding for people. I felt recognized. I was able to be who I was. There were no taboos. Mrs. Tweedie also sometimes gave me answers that were totally contrary to the usual or customary way of thinking.

Does an example occur to you?

Sure, but I don't really think it should be made public. You know that there was really no sphere of human existence which could not be addressed, that everything had a light shone on it, making it conscious. In every age there are collective values and behavior patterns that are under certain taboos, and Mrs. Tweedie sometimes pointed out, independent of contemporary moral values, something that would exactly touch the soul and the being of a person. She possessed a great openness in all questions. I never heard anyone ask something which was not met with understanding, from a human point of view. Of course in the process of spiritual training, if something came up that she needed to refuse at the moment, she did refuse it. For me, on the human side, she was as wide open as the sky. Everything really had space. That is a great quality that she had.

So at the beginning, I think until 1989, for about five or six years, I had a totally easy time. I heard stories from other people about how stern Mrs. Tweedie could be, but when I was there, strangely enough I never experienced that she threw someone out or that she was harsh with someone or put someone in their place. If, then there was a gentle reprimand.

During her visits to Switzerland I had two remarkable experiences with her. The first was that one time she asked me to meditate with her. That was at the very beginning when I met her. I lay down in the bed next to hers in the hotel room. And—I was simply gone. I think that was the first Dhyana experience that I had. She didn't say anything. I asked her, then, what that was, if I had simply been asleep. Although I somehow knew that I hadn't been asleep. But she didn't say much about it, didn't explain anything.

The other episode happened as we went to eat in a hotel. The restaurant upstairs, which was "normal", was closed and we were sent downstairs. There it was really rather elegant. We ordered the meal and then along came the waiter with a tray of bread. There were about five different kinds of bread on it and he asked us which bread we would like. Mrs. Tweedie got up abruptly and said that was absolutely decadent and ran out of the restaurant. I was understandably very shaken. Of course, I understood what it was about. We choked down the food and had received our lesson.

She went away by herself? You didn't go after her?

There was always a companion with her and she immediately went with her. I had no chance, I wasn't asked. Somebody had to pay the bill, on more level than one.

Inwardly, this phase was characterized by breaking up structures: to have fewer and fewer models at one's disposal, also to dissolve psychic structures which the ego could still hang on to. Actually one rug after the other was constantly being pulled from under one's feet.

Did you already have an awareness for this process or did you just experience how it happened?

I always observed what was happening. I didn't know anything about a spiritual way that was marked out. I really had no idea. I could never really listen during the talks because I somehow stepped away with my mind, so I actually knew very little. The complete book—*Daughter of Fire*—I did of course read; luckily it had appeared by then. Mrs. Tweedie had doubted for a long time whether a German publisher would appear for her complete diary *Daughter of Fire*, because it was so extensive, but finally a courageous publisher did say he was willing to issue the German version.

This book was my companion for fifteen years. I read it daily, from beginning to end and back to the beginning. In this way I gradually understood more and more. And my own process went on, and I just watched.

At first I experienced this dissolving, the removal of structures, the free fall. I noticed how the world faded, how it became gray. I felt the discrepancy between the inner world and the outer world. I turned towards the inner world without knowing how it was. I heard about this love that we would one day experience. I did not experience it. I think I experienced the desert. And that lasted a very long time. But I think that *in* the situation one always has the feeling that the desert is endless. In addition to that came this constant inner friction, which Mrs. Tweedie called the yo-yo principle. We'll talk about that later, for sure. There was a time at the beginning where I had a lot of dreams, too. They helped again and again. There was also a period of almost prophetic dreams, dreams in which I experienced the presence of saints, prophets, and teachers from other times and traditions. They also helped me very much. I began relatively soon to write to Mrs. Tweedie. Until the end I always wrote her everything. It was all the same to me whether I received an answer or not. I also tried to follow the principle of truthfulness in my letters—to really communicate everything, also my shadow sides. I also sometimes asked for advice or wrote her inner experiences.

I took Mrs. Tweedie's book very seriously. At the beginning she mentions the two masters over whose texts she makes an oath at the British Museum. I also went to the British Museum and asked to be given these writings. I sat there meditatively, contemplating these writings. And there was—and is—this connection. It isn't like Mrs. Tweedie told me a lot about what I should do. Actually, it wasn't like that at all. I read her book and then these particular steps followed by themselves, mirrored by this diary and from my own inner self.

So at the beginning you were with Mrs. Tweedie with a great ease and a kind of matter-of-factness. For each of us it was certainly different. And Mrs. Tweedie behaved totally differently toward each and every one, as well. She might have thrown someone else out who had such an easy-going attitude. Our experience with Mrs. Tweedie and how she dealt with us was completely distinct.

Yes, that's absolutely correct. If I had seen a stern side to her at the beginning, I would have been out of there. Mrs. Tweedie was, after all, nothing more than a mirror. And because I couldn't have stood it, it just followed that I was able to experience her like that during the initial phase. I think that had something to do with my being so reserved. I needed a lot of time before I could really trust. I had given the blank check; that was not the issue for me. But this inner, very delicate arena—this trusting from my innermost being and really opening myself—this took time. That has something to do with my alchemy. With her, I was recognized. Mrs. Tweedie was really just a mirror—but mirror is maybe not the right word. Her being was such that she was able to hold people in a spiritual way.

She knew what was inside of a person and found the way for it. If someone needed a certain tone, then she spoke in this tone. And with someone else it would be completely different. Like you said, that you would have gone away if you had seen the harder side of her earlier.

For me it was a unique combination—to be able to talk with her about everything, and to feel her presence. I was also often able to spend the night at her house. This slow opening of my soul that happened was really an unencumbered time for me with Mrs. Tweedy. But as I said, that was the beginning phase.

What came after that?

The turning point was the Sufi Camp in Hart, 1989, that George and I and some friends had organized and which proved to be extraordinarily difficult. We couldn't have anticipated it. At the end of this Sufi Camp, Mrs. Tweedie stuck me with the dagger, so to speak, and explained that I had embezzled money and that basically everything I had done for her was just not right. I remember exactly how and when this happened. It was at the end of the Camp. The house in which the events had taken place was not quite finished in some places, and Mrs. Tweedie stood on a kind of chicken-roost ladder in front of the entrance to the house and then she said all of this to me. She didn't say much at all, but it had such an effect. I was almost out of my mind. I no longer knew what was up and down, left and right. I was numb for two weeks. I could hardly speak at all. It was hell. The crazy thing was that I had already booked my next flight to London so that I could sit with her again in her living room for two weeks. She didn't totally throw me out—otherwise I would have broken to pieces over it. So I flew to London ten days later.

Was anything about this criticism justified? I mean, you wouldn't have embezzled any money.

No, I didn't—not a penny.

And you organized the Camp with all your energy and to the best of your ability and knowledge. You worked day and night with all your strength.

Mrs. Tweedie told me a year later that she had done that under the direction of Guruji, her teacher.

So I came to London. I could hardly pass through the door. It was terrible. I could no longer go into the main room where everyone else was.

Was that from your inner state of mind, or did she not let you in?

It all happened with relatively few words. I just didn't make it over the threshold. I wanted to, there was no question about that. But there was such an energy—I was like the leper, expelled. And the group went on in its lively way. Now I got to know the collective psychology of the group. Out of more than a hundred people in London, only three of them still spoke to me. Before this, everyone had been nice and friendly, and most of them knew me as part of the organization. But that turned around and with that the whole process became intensified. The group was also used, I suppose, to reinforce certain processes. Mrs. Tweedie insulted me some more in front of the group, saying that I had embezzled money and so forth. I could not say anything. It was like walking a tightrope over an abyss, really like walking on a bridge made of a single strand of hair. And there were moments where I actually did stand on a bridge and wanted to jump. It was an utter disaster for me.

It's perhaps important to say, at this point, that one takes criticism or being unjustly treated by a spiritual teacher much more to heart than when a partner or a colleague criticizes one, simply because one meets the teacher in such a deep place in oneself. It takes on a totally different dimension through the special relationship one has to the teacher.

Yes, absolutely. I mean, if one places all bets on one card, and I did do that, and that was the first time in my life that I'd done such a thing. Although for me the teacher did not signify the center—I had placed my bets on THAT. And Mrs. Tweedie was connected with this THAT. This was it, why one was able to be so deeply shattered. These are real dimensions that can hardly be understood with normal common sense. It has to do with this very deep opening, this most intimate inner opening of a person towards THAT. The teacher works on this level. There, in the deepest depths of the soul begins the shattering.

This is a different level than depression or feeling suicidal from a psychological point of view.

This is a totally different level. It is the essential level of one's very existence. It contains also the psychological dimensions but it reaches much deeper. It touches you at every level. And that is, I think, a huge difference. It goes into this dimension "Die and wake up!" And that goes far beyond the realm of psychology.

But—I couldn't jump. Mrs. Tweedie also talks about this in her diary. At that time she had been with her teacher for about a year; her training was particularly intensive due to the shortness of the remaining time. She also had the feeling that her teacher blamed her unjustly when he reproached her for not being loving enough, and for not being useful to him when he was sick. Mrs. Tweedie had been shocked, because she would not have dared to interfere in Indian family matters, and caring for a sick person is a family matter. After this accusation she was so desperate that she wanted to throw herself off the railroad bridge over the Ganges. But nevertheless, she had to go on this day to Guruji again; an inner sense would not let her do anything else. It was the day he looked at her, full of blinding light, and said to her that he knows the future of a person and *never* wastes his energy on anyone.

It becomes clear with this example that each person who walks this path passes through it in a unique way; and at the same time we recognize certain stages which are common to all.

When I read Mrs. Tweedie's book and knew that I would like to be trained exactly like that, I thought it would actually be impossible because the context is so different. But we do get trained in the same way, even if the form of expression for each person is unique and the context is different. But those points where it touches these deep existential levels, where it is about dying in order to live, those are gateways through which each one has to pass. And the training leads to that place where we get pushed in. We are lead into this corner. Imperceptibly, not consciously. If we would experience it consciously, we'd put on the brakes. The ego would get in the way. We are guided until we reach a point where we surrender. Totally give up.

I'd like to add something else, which certainly has to do not only with me but is generally valid. If we get repelled like that "in the world", if we get thrown out, most of the time we feel deeply hurt. In the process I have described here, *something* does not get hurt. And that shines through every difficulty, through the most extreme despair. In absolute misery emerges *something,* and one feels how a hand is there, which acts with love. That is a big difference to the usual sense of being thrown out.

There were two things, then, that happened which helped me. One of them was that I had a dream in which, on a symbolic level, the keys to my unconscious were given to me. That was a gift. Then, when I was so desperate I was almost unable to walk, suddenly, in a very real way, in the middle of the street, at home, there was a fragrance. And I knew it was no earthly fragrance. This perfume came from another world, and my heart knew it. It helped me to go on and to recognize love in everything. Everything. This is something that everyone experiences. Mrs. Tweedie said that when she throws someone out, she sends an angel after. This really does happen.

> Look, I died hundreds of times and learned one thing:
> When your scent came it enlivened me.
> And hundreds of times I sank into a swamp
> Then your call came and pulled me up again.
> I stretched out a net for the love-hawk
> My heart saw how it soared away![2]
>
> *Rumi*

It took me about a year to get somewhat balanced again. I continued going to Mrs. Tweedie as often as I could. I was on live coals every time. She didn't look at me for a whole year and one suffers unspeakably from such a thing. Not one glance for a whole year. It's really true that one can be totally shaken up by a frown from a teacher, or even if an eyebrow is raised. These dimensions are totally impersonal. It has nothing to do with Mrs. Tweedie as a person. It has something to do with empty space, with THAT. And it is an incredible grace when one is given the experience of this harshness, this depth, this mirror. It is the process of grinding and polishing a raw diamond, and this hurts. At the same time, it is the only thing in this world that makes sense. It's an invaluable phenomenon if one is able to find a path on which one can be lead Home. One can't appreciate it enough.

The Buddhists say there are three great blessings: to be born as a human being, to feel the longing cry in one's heart, and to find a path which will show the way Home. The human being does not need more than this—this is fulfillment.

So a second phase followed for me, one that was extremely difficult. I already had a meditation group at home. That was just happening—I was there for it.

I continued to go and see Mrs. Tweedie as often as possible, and when I was there with her I did not know who I was. To some extent I behaved like a two-year-old. I was fearful and yet I always had to go there. I was like another person. The others sometimes said to me: "You act so strangely. What is actually the matter with you?" Sometimes we, the Swiss group, were invited to tea with Mrs. Tweeedie. When this happened, I just sat there stiff as a board, with my knees clenched and a cup of tea in my hand, for two hours. I did not know what was happening to me. I noticed that I could hardly breathe. If Mrs. Tweedie looked at me, I'd turn red. It was horrible. Yes, and I was also proud. I talked very little in the group. It took a lot of effort to say anything. There, too, I was pressed so far that I couldn't do anything except open myself in front of the group. I cried, which is something I usually did secretly. Then I tried to be more courageous there as well, to just say things the way they were, to not hold back dreams, to expose myself over and over again.

In the meantime I had a little more space from the children so I sometimes went to London for three weeks. For me, this was a time in which I inwardly ran into walls. I bloodied my head, as it were, from this constant banging into the wall. I couldn't get anywhere. I didn't know what was going on. Only much later did that get resolved from a very deep level.

On the outer level, I gave up my third world work and only taught t'ai chi. I had more of a connection with t'ai chi. I had realized that aid work out there, far away from us, was one thing, but that aid work also had something to do with myself. I had understood that changing the outer structures is one thing, and the development of a person towards consciousness is another. I had understood that if we want to change the world, this change begins with myself and not with my neighbour—where it would be so simple, right? So, I experimented with myself, tried to change my ways of behaving and saw that I am a pretty tough nut to crack. A tough case. Which would take a while.

I just wanted to ask you if you were able to change your way of acting.

Certain things succeeded, but actually "succeeded" is the wrong expression. It was actually always something else that brought a change.

Isn't it actually more like something gets taken away? That in the end it happens from a different level, when change actually comes about?

Yes, that's right. It's quite an important experience to want to change oneself and to have to realize that it actually isn't possible. That also the whole reasoning principle that says, okay, now I'm going to do it—and all one's good intentions most of the time just don't hold water. To understand this is really helpful. And then to really experience with a deeper and deeper sinking-into-oneself and slowly forgetting oneself more and more, that things just gradually fall away. It gets done. I understood, too, that the world can only change in this way—it's not put on, it's not forced by some act of will—instead, it unfolds in a completely natural way from the inside. In the end, I attach value only to this way of becoming human. Everything else will tip over in an extreme situation. Everyone can test this for herself in everyday happenings.

Historically we have enough examples of how things manifest in extreme situations.

All the images that we construct of ourselves are attempts to somehow create ourselves. It's really about becoming how we were already created, how we really are. When we attempt on the path to also somehow try to "better ourselves", then that is an incredible misunderstanding that for one thing doesn't work and also brings an even bigger sense of estrangement. We miss this brightness implicit in our being which reveals itself when we open ourselves to becoming what we really are.

You say it very well. These are deep realizations, I think. That it's not about being this or that. It's only about being—being *what* we are. For me the process of realizing oneself is to say "Yes" to what is. To allow the unique fragrance to reveal itself. To sing the unique song, each in his or her own way. Or to allow the one tone to resound—this is what it's about.

Of course, this has to do with how one views the creation, what is actually meant with "creator", "creation". The way I see it today, the ONE mirrors itself in millions of forms, in an unbelievable variety. Every form and image, each facet and sound lives this uniqueness, with the knowledge within that it is only a reflection of the ONE. Because of this, I think it is wonderful to discover and live one's own being, without being identified with it. There is nothing else but THAT, the ONE. And each human being has the right to live his being, to allow her particular fragrance to unfold as part of the whole.

The Path II

I would like to say some more about the inner dimension of the path. When we say that the path of love is about a pathless path, the emphasis is that every turn of the path is unique. We don't speak much about so-called stages. In general, very little is explained. One allows the wanderer to have *experiences.* The accent is not placed on transmitting knowledge, rather that each person *experiences* for him-or-herself.

But I would like to roughly sketch what happens inwardly for nearly every person who walks this path, from an archetypal point of view. Stages were described, for example, by Teresa of Avila, in her *Inner Castle* as seven dwellings. We have similar images from Attar in his *Bird Conversations* with the seven valleys.

In alchemy, a process is described which begins with *Separatio*, in which separation takes place from the outer and inner world, from the world of appearance and the real world, the Ground of all Being. Among other things we learn to distinguish between light and shadow in ourselves.

This first stage of *Separatio* and the experience connected to it gradually leads to *Conjunctio oppositorum,* the union of opposites, the work of reconciliation. A spiritual path is reconciliation work. And that leads us finally into the *Unio mystica,* the experience of union, in which the lover and the beloved become one. It is characteristic of the Sufi path that we do not experience and keep anything for ourselves—also the *Unio mystica* is not for us. Everything happens only so that we will carry it back into the world through our being. In the end, it is about the experience that the outer and inner world, the world of appearance and reality are *not two.*

What is the difference between stages and states?

When we talk about stages, we mean a kind of general concept for orientation's sake, something that leads from A to B to C, like in the alchemical process we were describing before. Actually, though, a spiritual development or unfolding doesn't happen in a linear way. I said a minute ago that we speak very little today about stages, because in considering stages or steps a value often creeps in which, with the modern obsessive mentality of accomplishment and "getting somewhere", can be quite a hindrance. An example of stages can be seen in describing degrees of love. Bhai Sahib described these steps to Mrs. Tweedie in wonderful images: women carry jugs of water on their heads, they don't spill any water and they also don't break the pitchers. If one should happen to break, it is no big loss, one can get another. He demonstrates the second degree of love in the image of acrobats—they do take a risk but they use tricks to help them stay safe. In the third image he talks about insects which want to be the first to hurtle themselves into the light of a lamp.

The idea of stages or steps is really misleading. Development is like a spiral and we go through each stage in a new way on different levels. *And* it is a movement in its entirety that takes a person through each step, one after the other. But it can happen that suddenly a part that had until then been unnoticed appears suddenly in consciousness and goes through the steps from the beginning, while other areas of the person are already resting fully in love.

Within the different stages, if we remain with the idea, experiences are described in the tradition, which are characterized as states. Let's take as an example the yo-yo principle—these times of being inwardly uplifted, and then suddenly times in which great separation is experienced. Everything falls apart inside; one feels nothing except gray, like in the desert. Mrs.

Tweedie said that there is an awesome inner friction produced, first of all to bring the opposites with all their implications into consciousness, but also to generate the power to bring the opposites together. This path puts us under great psychic pressure. Perhaps in Zen, having to sit for hours at a time is the challenge for a person. For us—we sit less, as far as time is concerned—psychic pressure is the means by which we are truly put through the mill, where we are ground into dust.

The yoyo syndrome

The story about the name "yoyo syndrome" or "yoyo principle" is typical for how Mrs. Tweedie worked: it originated in her kitchen in a talk over tea. And then it held, because it described so graphically this change of mind states which people on the path experience.

In classical Sufi literature, a difference is made between *bast* (the yoyo is up) and *qabd* (the yoyo is down). These two conditions create a rhythm, a movement, they follow each other—not directly but in a kind of constancy.

Bast means, from its root, to become wider, to expand. God is near during these times. Mrs. Tweedie describes these states of joy—the one joy in which she could embrace the whole world and the other, which she silently feels in her heart. In this condition, poets celebrate the beauty of the divine lover: it is the condition one perceives inside as well as in the light of all creation.

Qabd means pressure. It is the pressure cooking of the soul, the great inner pressure under which the wanderer sometimes stands, where one "threads his home through the eye of a needle", as Attar describes it. We spend weeks, sometimes months in the desert, that "dark night of the soul", as John of the Cross calls it. It is difficult to bear because it represents the deep experience not only of darkness but above all the absence of a will, of one's own power, one's own possibility to act. We cannot do anything; nothing helps, no diversion, no explanation of our condition with, for example, the help of psychotherapy, as in a depression. This is a certain challenge for us westerners, who are totally habituated to constant action, to *doing*. "According to this system, the Shishya (disciple) gets constantly pulled back and forth between the opposites, between highs and lows. This creates the necessary friction to bring about suffering, which in the end conquers the mind."[1] The friction comes about through the "cleaning" of the heart; old impressions, experiences, images and ideas get swept out, as it were, so that the space of the heart becomes empty. This is empirically a painful process.

We've spoken now about stages and states; what other features of the path occur to you, that you find important to mention?

We have a high standard of ethics. Bhai Sahib gave Mrs. Tweedie several guidelines. But actually he taught more through his own example. It is an ethical sense that comes from silence, which grows from the heart. Which is not prescribed from outside, but rather which one becomes aware of—in the course of really growing up, of waking up to universal consciousness. One understands: if I hurt another, I am hurting myself. There is actually no real separation. But the ethical sense is really high—if one for example has one chair too many, something that one doesn't need, it is said that one is committing robbery, one possesses too much.

This sense of ethics is very alive, it arises from the presence of the heart. Quite different from morals, which establish set rules and stick to principles with no relation to the present situation. While you were talking, a story with Mrs. Tweedie occurred to me. It was in Eyendorf, at the first Sufi camp with her. There was a farm nearby and, accordingly, a lot of flies. Before we meditated, Mrs. Tweedie shut all the windows and killed the flies. Scandalized looks appeared, of course—what does that mean, to not hurt anyone, Mrs. Tweedie kills flies!—you know, all the pointing fingers. Then Mrs. Tweedie just said: "What's the higher good, the higher aim?" The higher aim was that those who were beginning with meditation—and we were all beginners at that time—could meditate in peace. The ethical sense is—different than morals—always in a lively flow.

*I*n that way it can happen that flies get killed. This is a very difficult issue, which demands great conscientiousness. In the Bhagavadgita there is a dialogue between Krishna and Arjuna, who is mulling over this question. It is about an action that leaves no trace behind, an action in which the I, the mine, is not operating. That is only something one knows *inside,* it isn't necessarily visible on the outside. The ethical sense is also different for each person according to his or her own sensibility.

Also in the situation?

In the situation and in one's sensibility. It is really true that each person needs to find out for her or himself what is right and what is not right. And that is not meant morally. But it requires a mature, conscious person. If you have immersed yourself in love, you cannot possibly infringe upon the fundamental human laws of ethics.

> Therefore renounce all fear and shame and all outer virtues. The virtue alone which you carry inside by nature, this you will want to find over and over, for eternity.[2]
>
> *Mechthild von Magdeburg*

Another distinguishing characteristic of the Sufi path—the "alone in the crowd" phenomenon—we already touched on indirectly in your life story.

I think that this is not only in our tradition, but that every mystic is "alone in the crowd". Everyone shares this. But we happen to call this condition "alone in the crowd". It's a feeling in life, a condition, which has to do with how one dies or is born. One is born alone and dies alone. We have another image too, which expresses a wonderful, mysterious experience: poverty of the heart. It is an inner state, an inner attitude in which we are open, vulnerable, present in the now in

HIS spirit. It contains a true humanity that feels, and at the same time this inviolable eternal part in a human being which can never be touched is shining brightly.

Mrs. Tweedie was in a position to transmit the timeless contents of the path to us in simple, practical instructions. For example: we first sweep in front of our own door. One sees the shadow sides of others so quickly, but most of the time these are mirrors of one's own shadowy parts. One can only change these parts in oneself. Of course we sometimes get angry with other people, but Mrs. Tweedie said, when it lasts longer than three minutes, then it has something to do with oneself. This path of love is really very practical; it contains such simple suggestions. If one really seriously carries through with them, one can learn an incredible amount. The path is practical—it's not aesthetic theorizing, but it is really about a way of life. Let's take another golden rule of Mrs. Tweedie: do that which brings you a step closer to God, and leave what takes you a step farther away from God. If one has a decision to make, it can be something big or something everyday, for example, whether I want to go see this film or not, then I look inside myself. In doing this, I get the feeling whether I want to compensate for something at the moment, or if I want to escape from myself—or if for example it is just time to play, time to relax. If a person listens inside, then he knows exactly what brings him closer to himself or farther away.

We people in this world experience all light and dark, up and down, times of suffering, times of pain, times of joy. In times of hardship, we are instructed to endure, just to see it through. That is generally one of the greatest qualities we need to learn on this path—endurance. In joyful times, when we are doing well, our heart is full of gratitude. Later, we feel gratitude for all states. We don't distinguish anymore between light and dark. One is more an observer, with a heart singing in silence. Gratitude is extremely helpful for inner development. Gratitude opens the heart. Nothing is taken for granted.

What do we know?

In essence, we really know nothing. Bhai Sahib emphasized this often and said, in essence we don't know. And this is really true. Not only Socrates but all the great teachers said: I know that I don't know. In our innermost depths we know nothing. In the end, Truth cannot be grasped. Everything that one can grasp with the mind is relatively gross. Truth escapes the possibilities of the mind. The heart can divine it, but there always remains something mysterious about it.

That's why we invent images and concepts, to at least attempt explanations.

On our path we possess for example a metaphysical understanding of how the creator allowed the creation to originate in an act of love. It is a union of love. The human being is born with this inner knowledge, this memory. In the course of growing up, she forgets what her real home is, what she really *is*. We learn through the experiences on the path to return to this source. Of course, the image of a union of love is also a concept. Everything which can be composed in words is not the Truth. It cannot be, since words are based on the principle of duality. Truth lies beyond. But words are a possibility for the human being to understand, and they help to move in a certain direction. They are like a bridge, a station of support. These words in themselves point to the truth, but they aren't the truth. Because this is nameless. Beyond the mentionable.

> The name which can be named is not the true Name.
>
> *Lao Tzu*

By the way, it is like this with everything that is in the world of appearances—everything points in itself to the Nameless. If one really looks—everything. We use the term "God" reluctantly.

Why?

Because in our culture the idea of God is very often related to an *image*. When we speak of the Beloved, we mean something that has no face, no name, no form. That may appear as a paradox if on the other hand we speak of the Lover and the Beloved. And it can just as easily be HER, by the way. I'm a woman and gladly assume the image of HIM. But in the end of course it is *the* Lover, and *the* Beloved. IT.

The Sufis have these incredible love metaphors, full of the richest, most voluptuous images.

Full of poetry, with gardens and roses and so on...

The rose is blossoming,
and the nightingale is drunk,
come, Sufis, come,
you who are devoted to wine!
The battlement of remorse,
as heavy as stone
in its laming solidity
look how the crystal goblet
effortlessly shatters it!
In this caravanserai
there are two doors to walk through:
The prize of love
is not to be won without pain.
O heart, do not wrangle about profit and loss,
in the long run it is really only Nothing
that waits for us at the end of every road![3]

Hafiz

***S**imilar to the "Song of Solomon".*

In the shadow of your curls
how sweetly my heart slept,
enraptured and full of love,
so peaceful, so free...[4]

Rumi

Yes, exactly.

***I**t's the same symbolism.*

Rose and mirror, sun, moon—what are they?
Wherever we gaze, only your countenance was to be seen.[5]

Mir

It conceals a kind of challenge. It's a big step on the inner way when this Beloved is no longer seen as an object or a form. In our culture this can produce a crisis for certain people, because this concept of God is so strongly embedded in us. This is an issue that affects our generation more than our children's. I grew up in a context that was full of images—God the Father, God the Son, God the Holy Ghost—these images are still strongly present in our culture. In this way, a picture appears almost automatically for most people when we talk of God, or Christ, for example. In this case the human being is here and the Divine is up there. When one has the inner experience that IT has no form, no name, no qualities, no face, then this psychological hold on an image or on help or comfort or hope just vanishes. There is nothing that we can hold onto, neither image nor name. This shakes one up inside, makes one feel quite precarious, really, because there is no solid ground anymore to stand on. One has arrived, but on the level of the world of appearance, the level of form, one cannot hold on to anything—nowhere, in fact, inherently and transcendentally. From the human and the psychological point of view, one's normal feeling for life gets deeply jolted. Every cell, every atom in oneself gets shattered. There is no longer the outside there and the inside here or God up there and the human being down here. Suddenly that all disappears. And the human being disappears with God. The union, the deepest reconciliation is a shock. This is not necessarily so for everybody, for some it is perhaps simply a kind of refined astonishment. When God dissolves into SOMETHING that just IS, then that is a great step.

The connecting of the two worlds doesn't only mean that we lead a normal life, work and have families, but there is a much deeper implication in this. It means that this separation between heaven and earth, between good and evil, between the holy and the profane in the final analysis just does not exist. In an obvious way, this means that the spiritual life is not separate from my "normal," everyday life. But like you just said, this refers in everything to IT, and that means bringing the two worlds together on a deep level. That's an aspect for me that really belongs in our time.

At the beginning of a spiritual journey we experience very often an incredible tension inside between the world of appearances, where we have problems, where we have disputes, where we are unsatisfied, and maybe also happy—but where the happiness may be suddenly taken away—and a spiritual world, which we feel as healing, as making ourselves whole. At first this can lead to an unbelievable tension in people through the *Separatio* because one doesn't understand at all how the two can connect.

In our latitudes this is of course strongly shaped by culture.

Very strongly.

In our Christian culture this separation was always pronounced. The one side was bedevilled. There was and still is a strong duality between the worlds—at the beginning you were talking about that from your time in the convent. So it seems to be something specific to our culture, that particularly at the beginning, we are so lost in this plunge into the other, the spiritual world.

That's right. It's hardly an issue in India because there the two worlds are much more strongly connected.

For us, spirituality is in general a difficult concept. We had the churches—when I was small there was the Catholic Church and the Protestant Church or one was Jewish or whatever. But there just wasn't much substance left in it, no real spiritual understanding. And today the churches stand empty in many places. Through the natural sciences with their rational attitudes towards the world, spirituality has shifted farther into the background. Although today another movement is emerging; the natural sciences are delivering, so to speak, the material for a new spirituality. But to begin with, we are experiencing a great split. What is at stake is to dissolve this split in oneself, to stop making separations between inside and outside, between above and below. But in the end one cannot *do* this; it just happens, it is given to one.

Still, effort is needed. Yes, at the beginning, the wanderer has to exert a lot of effort. A certain care is needed, a certain alignment. Eventually, a point comes where it gets easy.

When we look closely, we can easily understand this. Take, for example, someone who has never meditated and begins to, every day for three-quarters of an hour: that is not much time in relation to the twenty-four hours of the day. If one dedicates three-quarters of an hour a day to the Higher Self, to the Nameless, that is actually very little when one considers that it is our own essence. But at the beginning, even this three-quarters of an hour is quite an effort, one needs to surmount obstacles; perhaps for several weeks it requires real discipline. Then one notices how it slowly becomes a necessity. How this sitting becomes a spring at which the nourishment of the soul takes place. This is basically true for the whole path: that at the beginning one has to exert effort, but later it works easily. It is a need, to devote oneself to IT. One is nourished and carried. And it becomes very light.

The ocean comes for the dewdrop. It is not that the dewdrop falls or flows into the ocean.

> The seventh Poverty a Nothingness—
> And there you are suspended, motionless,
> Till you are drawn—the impulse is not yours—
> A drop absorbed in seas that have no shores.[6]
>
> *Attar*

It is the Beloved who unites itself with the Lover, not the other way around. What we learn through our practice is to slowly open—to slowly, like wax, melt into something higher. Into the Beloved. It is a process in which things just fall away. Like an onion, whose layers slowly come undone. Things that were important simply become unimportant. We are moved to less and less. It is an automatic process. Automatic is perhaps not the right word, it would be better to say an organic process. Like when a plant, a flower, slowly pushes through the ground, grows into the springtime, opens her blossoms.

For me it was always something special that we had a love relationship to the Divine, to the Nameless. This moved me deeply, it touched me. I come from the Christian tradition and there was God the Father, God the Son, God the Holy Spirit—Holy Spirit wasn't at all clear to me, what that actually was—and this was a reference to something quite far away, somewhere. Here in the circle of the Sufis we speak of the Beloved, and that is the most heartfelt, intimate relationship which is possible to have. The human being is in a love relationship with the Divine; this inspired me deeply, this filled my soul.

We work on the Atmic level on our path. Spiritual life means a quickening; as a matter of principle, only the heart chakra becomes activated. Our path works only with the heart chakra, that is enough for us. And afterwards, the whole alchemy is unfolded, so to speak, which constitutes the process of becoming whole.

The heart chakra becomes activated—can you elaborate on this?

When we come together and meditate, go into silence, then someone may suddenly feel a heart palpitation or sometimes also a kind of stabbing in the heart. Through this vessel, through this kind of meditation, through the *dhikr,* the heart chakra becomes quickened. Spiritual life means that the human being orients him or herself to a higher frequency. We get accelerated, and through the acceleration all kinds of possible and impossible things turn up. We have to work it out, integrate it in order to become whole, in order to recognize, in the end, who we really are—IT. But—who are we, to name IT?

The Love Affair

What is surrender?

Surrender is nothing more than the one step back from oneself. To let be what is. And what is, is divine. It embraces heaven and earth. It simply embraces everything.

At the same time it is the greatest joy. For me it is the love affair. If one can look from the point of view of an observer, then the creation reveals itself in its entire multiplicity. In its fullness. Mrs. Tweedie often said: "Each person is unique. The artist does not paint the same picture twice. Each one is unique." In this I feel so much love and such a richness, such a beauty. It is overwhelming. In this way it becomes understandable that each person is loved on his own account. Not because he does this or that, but rather he is loved for how he is. And how he was, before he was. This is the love affair.

In the time when I had gotten the blow from Mrs. Tweedie, I came under an incredible inner pressure. Everybody on the path experiences this sometime. It gets down to the original split inside of one. Every person carries within a feeling for wholeness, for entirety, for undivided love, for the One. We all carry IT in our hearts.

We are born into this world and at some point we experience a separation, because this world of appearances is based on duality. That's often the point at which we no longer feel loved, we feel rejected, not accepted. Most of the time it is an unconscious process, a deep inner shock. We start to identify with this because we take this world to be real. It's a kind of nuclear split. How we react to this "nuclear split"—and also the split itself—needs to be made conscious.

For example, I felt from the earliest childhood that I was not accepted. My shadow reaction to that was to do as many good things as possible in order to get this love, this attention, to experience this being accepted. This is not just a personal matter; it is almost archetypal. One can observe how this pattern extends itself through very different aspects of life. Of course I had always hoped that Mrs. Tweedie would accept me. But as a matter of fact, she didn't just cover over this wound: quite the opposite, she threw me into it once again. Through this, I became aware of this core injury and with that a deep healing was able to take place.

As an inner image during meditation, I held myself in my arms like a child, embracing myself tenderly. In this way, I experienced symbolically how we are truly loved in our such-ness and that love can never come from outside but can only be found in ourselves.

The experience of love flowed slowly through my whole being. A veil was lifted. I understood deeply how the whole of creation is nothing other than love. It is an enormous release when we experience this. One doesn't have to project it outwardly anymore and expect to be loved by others. But more than anything, there is an inner sense of fulfillment, a sense of being carried, a light singing. It is purely an inner process, independent of outward events, that reflects itself later on the outside—not in the way that outside circumstances necessarily change, but in the way that we perceive the world of appearances. What else could one want? It is really an enormous liberation, a grace. The greatest gift that can be given to a human being. Because then one is free.

This aspect is also essential to Mrs Tweedie's book, and many on the path experience this. This is the promise in the arena of love, to experience this love in the process of "die and become". For me it happened gradually, gently and delicately. Love has a thousand faces and each person will experience them in his or her own way. This love is divine nourishment. With this one can truly live. And with this, I would say, life begins. Die and become. It has to do with this.

Then I felt something deep within—at first imperceptible, after the long desert time. At first it happened in my innermost being, then later, in a further phase, in the outside world. I already have spoken about how development begins here, for each of us. Changing the world can only come about from the inside of a person.

But I didn't know what it was. As if a fruit was getting slowly over-ripe and was about to fall. But it didn't fall and didn't fall. Somewhere inside was a pushing and crowding, but I didn't know what it was. This happened during the heavy time about which I was speaking earlier.

In the winter of 1990 it broke through vehemently, and it became clear to me that I was to do this work which I am doing now. I had never thought of something like this before. It had been beyond imagining for me. It came out of the clear blue sky.

I wrote to Mrs. Tweedie and she immediately wrote me back. "Yes, so be it. Get started!"

That was the beginning of this "work", and for me it was simply It. I had arrived. That was a great turning point. With that also all the dreams, these almost prophetic dreams, stopped. This was an inner cut, an inner change.

From then on I was also free again towards Mrs. Tweedie. There was still a quiet fear, but access was possible again. I experienced an incredible amount of support from her until the end. She helped me immensely. I was able to ask everything, endlessly ask. I went to her until her death, every month for three or four days. It was yet another phase that I was able to experience with her.

Her illness, her broken femur, also happened during this time. The breakdown of her bodily strength began. She had once said, "For those who see how I slowly disintegrate, it is a great opportunity". For us in this connection, it meant a further growth in the sense that we became, spiritually speaking, adults. On the one hand to see her human condition, how the body falls into ruin; and at times her mind wasn't quite clear either. To bear this with the great example in our hearts, with concepts and expectations towards a teacher, also with our projections...It was a time in which I had to withdraw the last projections onto the teacher; I got to learn what was human and what was divine in human beings. Also to see the small without losing sight of the large. And on the other hand, to allow the large its true greatness and to accept the small as part of human existence, to accommodate it. Mrs. Tweedie always did show her human side. That was something that I experienced, during the time that she still received the group, as very beneficial. Because she let us take part in her process, in her perception and understanding, in her own further growth. She also never labelled herself as a teacher. She always referred to Bhai Sahib, her teacher. Through her opening up, for example, that she was afraid of the eye surgery, of great pain, of the blindness that was threatening, the fact that she communicated these things to us, letting us take part in them, made her accessible to us as a human being. She was not above the personal, not beyond the attainable. Not beyond the fact that we too could some time become whole or complete. It was a great talent of hers to let us be a part of that. But at the end, when just a few people were allowed to go to her, it was still another dimension. There it was really about disintegration and decay. To look at that, to bear it and then along with it to experience these absolute moments of light in an intensity and magnitude, these next to each other and with one another—that was quite a deep teaching. I would consider that today as becoming spiritually mature. In that way she got us ready to really be rooted in our own light. She very often quoted the last words of Buddha to me: "Follow your own light, Ananda." She told me that over and over again.

This time was very, very precious for me. I was able to ask her a lot of things about my "work", and what concerned me in my own growth. To the very end I felt Mrs. Tweedie to be the most beautiful person I have ever encountered. In spite of her 92 years, her face, her eyes, her hands were sometimes so saturated with light that it almost took my breath away. And the silence, when we meditated together—we sat together in meditation until the end—it had such a quality, of endless depth. One cannot really describe it. This silence with her was beyond naming. I owe her so much. What remains is deep respect and love. My heart is at her feet.

The Teacher

What role does a teacher play?

Today a certain development of this pathless path is making itself visible. Still, the issue of teacher remains a big one, not only on our path. I think it's important to also understand this aspect from the right point of view. First of all, the teacher is nothing other than a guide. Everyone who goes on a spiritual road has to walk it him-or-herself. It is a path for adults. The responsibility remains to a large extent with the one walking it. We don't have many outer instructions. The wanderer has to look into herself, she has to initiate certain steps, she needs to adopt the discipline that is necessary. That is the outer aspect.

Inside there is a lot of help. The teacher is the vessel for that. There are many things that happen on the path that we cannot explain, which are mysterious. In the end, what the disciple does do for himself is marginal compared to what is given to him. The teacher is a kind of focal point, a catalyst. The teacher is the mirror, is someone who can help when mystical experiences happen that can't be explained in this world. When inner worlds reveal themselves, open wide or collapse, the human teacher is there to help.

I think that the teacher's function has also changed over the course of time. We don't even know the name of Bhai Sahib. His example is unprecedented. We also didn't experience him, I didn't know him. He lives through the testimony of Mrs. Tweedie. It lives in us. With Mrs. Tweedie we were allowed to call her by name.

But only by her last name.

Only by her last name, but we were allowed to address her that way. I think something is reflected in that too, and that is that the teacher is coming nearer to the disciple—as a phenomenon of our time. The distance is apparently diminishing. Maybe, too, humanity in general is in an evolutionary process in which it is slowly growing up and in this way the distance between teacher-disciple gets a different latitude.

You are being called even by your first name.

A further step. It is never about the *person* with the teacher, that's a very central point. He or she is the empty space that points to the empty space in the disciple. At the beginning, the teacher is something on the outside that points to the inner teacher. The aim of the training is that the human being lives his light. In the end—in a way—he leaves the teacher behind, he leaves the path behind. In Zen they say, "Kill the Buddha when you meet him."

Too little projection on the teacher might not be enough; too much projection on a teacher can be harmful. Most of the time a disciple moves through a process in which she sees embodied in the teacher that for which she feels an endless longing. The teacher bridges over this projection, so to speak—carries it—so that trust can stabilize in the disciple. Trust in this light which the disciple ultimately carries in herself and which is mirrored through the teacher. At the appropriate time—sometimes it becomes visible through dreams, sometimes it happens by itself—the projection has to be withdrawn, because the teacher is nothing other than a resource, a guide.

As though he would give the disciple the address, when he is looking for a certain Home. Like a mountain guide, he knows the territory and says, "Go over there; now turn off to the left; careful, here comes an avalanche all of a sudden, wait a moment, stand still." If the disciple has arrived, these instructions are unnecessary. We do not revere a teacher, we respect him from the bottom of our hearts and are full of gratitude. But we *bow* only to the ONE.

It is important to me to put this in the right perspective because there is a lot of uncertainty these days in this area. For me, Mrs. Tweedie is guide and model, as far as teachers are concerned. She never labelled herself as teacher. I always felt free. It is in accordance with the tradition to give the disciple the greatest possible freedom. There was never an obligation of a personal nature in any way. She was an empty page, a white page, empty space. That was it. Few directions. The way in which she led people is exemplary for me. It was simply empty space, and for me this is the highest form of teaching. Real training happens in silence. Words can be very helpful, but the actual teachings take place in silence. This is the most powerful form of teaching. Mrs. Tweedie told us that we meet in the night, and that there the actual training happens.

In her book, in her journal, Mrs. Tweedie passed on some quite essential things, carrying them forward, as it were, like a torch. I know someone who was in Ladakh two years ago and met Sufis there who knew Bhai Sahib. These were Naqshbandiyya Sufis. They characterized him as a great illuminated teacher.

It is particularly remarkable that he gave the continuation of the Naqshbandiyya Mujaddidiyya Sufi lineage to a woman. That is extraordinary when one looks at the context. Three years ago I had access to a letter, in which a Naqshbandi teacher from Uzbekistan wrote in relation to Mrs. Tweedie, that a woman could never carry forward the Sufi teachings. So it's still not a given that the sexes are treated equally. One finds that also in Buddhism or when one looks at our church—there are still no Catholic women who are priests. We see this pattern everywhere. But Bhai Sahib did it differently.

There is still something else which impresses me about his quality as a teacher: he condensed the essence of the teachings to such a degree that the specific peculiarities of the path get overridden and he introduces something else—he said—there is nothing but nothingness. I see in this the onset of a universal spirituality, as all direct experiences of God find their place in this statement. This will be extraordinarily important for the development in today's world. With this he made a statement, and Mrs. Tweedie passed it on. It is to her credit that she was able to grasp it at that time and then pass it on to us. Master Eckhart with his "nameless road" says exactly the same—God is nothing.

> Whoever talks about God in any kind of parable talks in a dishonest way about him. But he who talks about God as nothing or everything talks to the point. When the soul comes into Oneness and within this enters into pure abandonment of itself, it finds God there as though in a nothing.[1]
>
> *Master Eckhart*

I know the Buddhist tradition a little; it's similarly formulated there.

With this we arrive in the dimension of the basic experience of being human, where the point is to be a human being, not just Sufi or Christian or Hindu, but human. It's a path that's as old as humanity and here a circle is closing. Here, we are coming to a cosmic religion, an interdenominational spirituality.

***What** do you mean by cosmic religion, or interdenominational spirituality?*

That first of all a dialogue between people begins, people who may have been able to experience the Ground of all Being and with this are at home in universal consciousness. From this dialogue, from this exchange perhaps a language will be found through which the Essential can be clearly and lightly expressed. It is a process—beyond institutions—that will be set in motion.

I just see this particular development on our path and on others that much is getting peeled away, so to speak. What was specific to culture or was carried historically at times is falling away more and more and we are advancing relatively quickly to the core practice. I think that every path must have a kind of core practice. And I could imagine that a cosmic religion puts them together and makes them available to people who then choose themselves which is more appropriate for his or her own inner alchemy. The only purpose is that the person realizes himself and with that, IT—how he does this is actually secondary. Which doesn't mean that it isn't a difficult process, one that must be carried out carefully and with deep reflection. The essence of the path has to be preserved.

We are certainly still very much at the start. The first thing could be that an exchange happens at a deep level, a dialogue, and not only an inter-religious one in which each lineage stands next to the other and gets recognized; rather it should go deeper, perhaps through common meditation and exact insights about what helps the person be able to recognize herself in a simple and straightforward way.

That's something that is happening today. We Sufis say that there are three journeys—the journey *from* God, in which we've forgotten who we really are, who IT is. Then the memory of the love affair, the path of love, that is nothing more than the journey *to* God. Then there's another threshold, where the journey *in* God happens. And about that, so far, little has been said.

Because nobody is there anymore who returns from there.

No. It wasn't the time. It was not yet the time. I think that there is also a kind of delicate language possible at the threshold when one comes back. It is a language that is universal. Guruji had spoken it. Mrs. Tweedie put the accent on the journey *to* God.

And the journey *in* God is getting more and more significant. Wasn't it said by Karl Rahner, Ayya Khema and others that if the human being does not become a mystic in the twenty-first century, humanity will not survive. That may or may not be, but in any case we're standing at a crossroads in the evolution of humanity. Jean Gebser divided the history of human beings into individual steps in consciousness. In his view of things, we are now coming out of a linear mental level of consciousness into contact with a universal or transpersonal consciousness—the terminology is still open—in which we experience inwardly that we are not separate; which means that we experience the all-one consciousness, which manifests in each being, in every appearance of the world. This dimension has to do with the journey *in* God. This is the next step that will find a language, an expression. This is already laid out in Mrs. Tweedie's book. It is like a shining star.

But in the very end we have to leave everything behind us. There are neither disciples nor teachers, neither a path nor anything that one can actually name.

A Living Tradition

Last night an image came to me how the rivers of the mystical traditions make a kind of net over our whole earth and beyond. Sufismus—the nameless path—has a kind of "color" which attracts certain people, in which certain people feel at home. I think now we will pick out a few points that make this tradition what it is.

Yes, that's a good idea. The same thing actually happened in the night for me. I saw a wheel: The outer circle is the human being who most of the time goes around and around here, when he has no path and no direction which lead him to himself. But what we want to talk about now are the spokes that lead into the empty space—the hub. This is the task of every mystical path and it has to be defined, of course—between outside and hub—in this domain.

The priority of our path is the experience of truth. It is a pathless path, a mystical path. Now, when we consider this spoke, the color is golden yellow, the note "D", and behind that is a tradition; this means that there is a line from master to master to master in which the knowledge, the wisdom teachings are passed on. It is the path of love. First I said that a Sufi is someone who is nobody. My second answer is that a Sufi is a lover. Characteristic of our path is that it is a silent one, it works out of the silence; the whole practice happens in silence. The meditation is a yogic practice to make the mind become still; it is an immersion into love. Because of this it is called the path of love. We sink into it and forget ourselves.

The second practice is the mantra, the *dhikr.* That also is practiced in silence; from the outside nobody can see if it's being practiced or not. It is one word—*Allah*—that most people on this path say as *dhikr.* It's interesting that the Dhyana meditation stems more from the Indian/Hindu tradition. Our Naqshbandi branch, the Naqshbandiyya Mujadiddiyya came to us by way of India. The oriental legacy is even more visible in the *dhikr. Allah* is an Arabic word, is older than Islam, and in its most intrinsic meaning it means *nothingness.*

Dhyana Meditation

Dhyana is a Sanskrit concept and means sinking, the turning off of all impressions coming from outside and of the inner processes of perception. This meditation is therefore a practice to empty the consciousness, or mind; in the Christian tradition it is recognized as the highest contemplative practice. The instructions for this are very simple.

There is no definite bodily posture, so one can practice this meditation whether one is healthy or sick. The important thing is that the body is relaxed.

We turn our attention inside, going deep into our innermost being.

We become still. Diving into the feeling of love, we sink into it body and soul. Our entire being is received in love.

Then there will probably be thoughts that appear, memories and images. And in our imagination we take hold of these thoughts and emotions and drown them in love.

Love is the highest power in the whole universe; it has the ability to turn everything into itself.

So the vehicle is conceivably simple. Another characteristic of our path is that the people on it are engaged in life. We have jobs, families, we're quite normal people. We don't seclude ourselves and don't wear any special clothing.

Add to this the teacher. He is the focus. First I addressed the vehicle because it is possible that a disciple has little access to the teacher—for whatever reason, maybe that she lives too far away, or has responsibilities that make it impossible to see the teacher often. Sometimes one encounter is enough.

My experience is that *every* way that a disciple undertakes seriously will lead to the goal. I am absolutely convinced about that. The earnestness and sincerity of the disciple or wanderer or pilgrim is of central significance.

What we use on our path additionally is the dreamwork; this has a long tradition. Dreamwork is a wonderful instrument. Earlier in the Sufi tradition stories were often told by way of example to explain situations to people, to make them understandable. Today, the dreamwork has taken over this function, in part.

In the dreamwork something similar happens like in the stories—it is not taught directly. The teacher talks to the door and means the window. On the one hand this is mysterious; on the other hand it expresses a deep respect for the person. The teacher doesn't say, you have to learn this or that by now but instead it's said through the dream symbol or the story. Or the teacher says something to someone else and if one has ears to hear—like you emphasized, a path for adults—then at that moment one hears it loud and clear, and one knows exactly: ah, that was meant for me.

That's true—this deep respect, this love for the person expresses itself mysteriously in this way. The person is loved and respected without limit for that which he is. The dreamwork is used today as well in this way. It's actually a work of genius the way Mrs. Tweedie took over the dreamwork, introduced it to the group and intensified it. It had been there with Bhai Sahib already—it's been in the tradition for a long time—but Mrs. Tweedie had studied C. G. Jung and she saw the development in the West. She saw people's interest in psychology, in wanting to understand inner processes, something that went hand in hand and could be used for this work. The dreamwork means confrontation with one's own shadow. No spiritual way can omit working with one's shadow. The point to our dreamwork is reconciliation with the shadow. Oftentimes people have negative associations with "shadow-work" but after all, this is the mud out of which the lotus flower can grow. Because precisely in this shadow realm the greatest treasures are found.

I myself haven't studied psychology but sitting for years with Mrs. Tweedie and listening to the dreams have given me a deep insight into the unconscious of people—not only in the unconsciousness—but in the real power of the person at the core. Every single person possesses a unique dream language—by the way, this is another characteristic of our path; we say, there are as many ways to God as there are breaths of the human being. The distinctness of a person is deeply respected and this is reflected in the dream language. If one watches this over a certain period of time, one also sees how the person changes. He receives access to worlds in himself that he can discover through dreams. She acquires an instrument to get to know herself, that I find really wonderful. Because the dreamwork happens in the group, many others are allowed to have a part in it.

And it provides a framework. Meditation takes place before the consideration of dreams, so an atmosphere arises which is allowing and open; and through that the dreamwork gets a very special quality. It is a sanctuary where every person can show him or herself as they are. With all of the faltering steps, with the shadows and the treasures which are often hidden in the unconscious.

***It** is a fundamental characteristic of this way to be "modern", which means up to date with the times. Through Mrs. Tweedie's book we can see three generations now and are astonished over and over at the rate of change. Bhai Sahib had to observe all the* *rules and forms of respect for his teacher; for example, how one enters or exits a door. In spite of this, for his time it was absolutely "modern" that he as a Hindu came to a Muslim teacher. Mrs. Tweedie's training with Bhai Sahib already signified an enormous change compared to how he himself was taught by his teacher. Then how we learned with Mrs. Tweedie and how it is now—it always happens in time, always rising to the demands of the time. Without losing an iota of the essential.*

Adapting to an era, to the cultural and social conditions, is necessary. This is how it happened that dreamwork stepped in front of story-telling. We live in a time in which, with the help of a contemporary science—psychology—dreams are dealt with; telling stories, though, is no longer deeply rooted, we're more a cognitive society. What needs to be communicated on the path to realization remains untouched by this outer change.

Quite another societal, cultural and religious context existed in India than with Mrs. Tweedie in London or in America, or in Europe. Things change and the *zeitgeist* changes. Accommodation takes place but without losing the essence. In this way the path is lively, a living tradition.

Is there a difference in the training between men and women?

Yes, the difference in the training of men and women is conveyed by Bhai Sahib in Mrs. Tweedie's book. The men receive more practices to transform their power, while with the women the concentration is on love—for the purpose of overcoming attachment. Energetically, men and women are different. This is clear and rests on the principle of polarity. The soul, on the other hand, is neither male nor female; the inner principle is beyond man or woman.

Today, though, a certain development is appearing in our society. More and more we are seeing that each woman connects her feminine side and her masculine side and lives both, and that also the man recognizes and integrates his masculine and feminine sides. Traditionally we say that the woman contains everything in herself. She needs only love to dissolve her attachments. The man has to transform his power. That's the traditional statement. For some people that is still true today, so the training is handled differently. But I see in today's world a shift, where men have to integrate the feminine and women the masculine. If, for example, a woman these days has more masculine parts, then of course the aspect of the training that has to do with transformation of power steps more into the foreground. Actually, every person is unique. Today I would say that the training happens according to the unique alchemy of the respective person. That is also tradition.

Why do you say that there's a certain shift happening?

It was stated in Mrs. Tweedie's book that sexuality was to be transformed in the last stage. That really got my attention. I often asked Mrs. Tweedie if I should stop being together now with my husband. I wanted to give up really everything for this path. Then I found out that for us women it's not such an issue to begin with, because—this is what Mrs. Tweedie said—the substance necessary to carry out the transformation of the heart is already there in the woman. In spite of that I kept asking, yes, but how is it, how is it then? And I understood that for me as a woman it just wasn't necessary. When I began with my "work", I asked again—how is it for men? I never got a definite answer. But sometimes she kind of threw in, because this question came up again and again from the other side, that today the transformation is no longer compellingly necessary, for men either. I don't know. I only know how it is and was for me. I think something is changing. Maybe it has to do with the fact that there are two trends, at the moment, concerning sexuality. On the one hand, the split is getting more extreme, violence and brutality are on the rise; on the other hand, sexuality is no longer being experienced as something split off, but rather as something healing, sacred, where body and spirit come together as one.

On the deepest level, the sexual act is a sacred act. Mrs. Tweedie said that the creation arose out of an act of love. Somehow this is reflected in the human meeting of man and woman. Of course, new life comes from this. I think that if we can bridge and reconcile the split between body and soul which took place in the Christian tradition since the late antique era—this split between spirit and matter, man and woman—when we understand that the one is not high and the other low, when we can see and experience sexuality as something natural, bestowed on us by creation, then this issue is transformed. And of course sexual energy is a strong energy, a part of the kundalini energy; but today I also know that the kundalini energy is not developed in all people in the classical way described by the Indian kundalini yoga teaching. So I don't believe that it's absolutely necessary that the sexual power has to be transformed for realization—meaning that one must renounce sexuality. Mrs. Tweedie indicated this two or three times in my presence. But we also need to watch and simply listen inside for answers to this.

The Group

Let's *talk about the group.*

Yes.

The *first thing that occurs to me is that in the group there is this special, subtle/powerful atmosphere which one can't describe, but which one senses immediately on coming into the group. It's not conspicuously "holy", like we know it from our cultural background. We laugh, we exchange recipes, tell jokes. The atmosphere gets broken again and again.*

No, the atmosphere doesn't get broken; the subtlety is always there, only the surface stuff gets broken.

So *that nothing too disengaged from the world comes about.*

Yes, it's really like that. It's like my first encounter with Mrs. Tweedie. In the group it's exactly the same. We drink tea, eat cookies and cakes and there are human conversations. Sometimes there's something incredibly funny, sometimes there is also something to cry over—it's normal life. It is just not separated.

In *this defined space of the group where one goes to meditate and pray, where the Unnameable is often so present as if one could touch IT, the "other" world is also part of it.*

Yes, because Sufis don't deny the world in its essence, but instead they enjoy it in the sense that they notice beauty and majesty, the female and male aspect and integrate them in their everyday life. They don't turn away from these things; but everything has its place. What was created cannot be bad. The whole person, the whole of creation—big and small, a bit crooked, a bit off, in its abundance and sometimes also stingy—everything has its place. I only wish I had more humor…

You *mean yourself?*

Well, Mrs. Tweedie used to tell jokes sometimes and I just have such a hard time remembering them.

It is like that—cheerfulness and humor are a central issue. In the end we have to learn to laugh about ourselves. That is liberation. Everything is not so serious. What happens in this world is really a play, HIS play, HIS mirror, HIS reflection. And in essence nothing can happen to us. Once we've experienced this, then a standpoint is possible for us that really can be humorous and joyful, that can also have tears; but essentially we know, it is HIS play. In essence, nothing happens, nothing at all.

What also happens in the group, which we already talked about in another way, is that teachings happen indirectly. One receives few, if any, direct pointers. It is more that "something" happens in the group surrounding the teacher, from which we learn. This is as true in the group as in the life we live "outside". Sometimes we sit there and look at the teacher with big eyes, waiting for him or her to come out with something wise, and ask ourselves, when is the teaching finally going to be for me? And right then somebody bumps me with their foot in my back and all my anger arises—and there is where the teaching happens. So not in this direct contact but in the occurrences in the group surrounding the teacher. IT occurs. And the perfectly appropriate situations always come. Or if I think that I've understood something, that I've gotten through some issue, then someone comes along in the group who challenges me to such a degree that I have the feeling I haven't learned a thing on this path. Or something happens, like this summer with this bird's nest—during the construction phase, when all the windows were left open, a family of birds settled in—and some people felt disturbed by their "noise" or just on that day the children come along and "disturb" the atmosphere.

The day the bird's nest was finally gone.

I can only verify this from my own experience with Mrs. Tweedie. The issues came to a head with enormous speed. How quickly I noticed all my projections that I then had to take back. If we look closely, the exact same thing happens in our everyday life. Mrs. Tweedie always said that life is the greatest teacher. It becomes a full-time job when we learn to pay more and more attention to this language of life. It is really a 24-hour activity because, seen with a deep understanding, the things that happen outside represent a reflection of an inner condition. With this, we are given a chance to become conscious of the aspect that can be read from it. Later, this full-time job becomes, in the deepest sense, joy; one is the observer and more and more recognizes quite simply HIS play. There is no longer any good or bad, one is natural and spontaneous, totally in the now, without the I or the mine getting in the way. And this is not accomplished and done with at a certain point; this is always new, in every timeless moment.

I have the impression that now, after the death of Mrs. Tweedie, the meaning of the group is dropping away, that more responsibility is being transferred to the individual again. Basically, it's similar to the time when we started out. At the beginning, there weren't many groups with Mrs. Tweedie. Many of us were quite alone.

I think you are right. For me it's clear that it's going more into individual responsibility. Today we are at the point where we have become more skillful in our self-understanding—for example, that we can relate things that happen to us "outside" to our inner life. This is of course connected to a bigger independence in being able to practice this conscious learning in everyday life.

There are groups in Germany, Switzerland and America that meet regularly. The groups are quite open, one comes together to meditate and at the same time remains free. At the beginning, especially, it is really a help to have a structure where one has the feeling, "Ah, yes, here I am allowed to really *be*, here I can find a piece of Home." This feeling-oneself-mirrored is important. Many people, though, don't like any group at all.

Because those who feel drawn to this path are actually loners?

They are loners.

There's a contradiction here in itself, to feel good in a group.

Exactly. Everything that manifests has two sides. A group can of course also develop a shadow side, a collective side. Suddenly a big part of the group dreams, for example, of certain indefinable dark energies. They get projected outwards and it escapes them—because there are so many—that it's still about their own parts. This unconscious process can develop an enormous dynamic of its own. One needs to be very attentive to how a group really functions. Because of this, once in a while Mrs. Tweedie would also suspend the group; she closed the door and was just gone for a time. One of the reasons might have been such a dynamic; certainly there were others as well. By the way, the path too possesses a shadow side; every path has a shadow side—like every person, as long as he lives, will be confronted with shadow sides, because it corresponds with the principle of duality. Every path has its strength, is a piece of cake that the person finds appetizing, but it also includes a shadow side. I think that one of the possible shadow sides of our path could be—in general for the Sufi tradition—the role of the teacher. It is really on the razor's edge. In her book, Annemarie Schimmel wrote about Sufi orders in which abuse took place. That's a point that must be looked at very carefully.

***It's** a balance between submission and freedom.*

And responsibility for yourself. In spite of this, one needs to listen exactly to what the mirror reflects. For me, Mrs. Tweedie performed this with mastery, that I have to say. For me she is a great example. She gave the disciple freedom; I never felt in any way obligated or immature, I always had to verify things for myself. The actual process begins with learning to really listen if the teacher says something. *Really* listen. Because most of the time we only hear within our known concepts. One has to develop the capacity—being as empty as possible—to simply listen. Then the words need to be tested. Deeply tested, contemplatively. Only then will it become clear in one's own heart what is right for one. This too is something one needs to learn: to handle this in an adult way. It needs much differentiation and a balance on the razor's edge, also for the disciple, so that he is true to himself, in his heart—I'm speaking about the heart. But he also has to really listen and take seriously what is said, absolutely seriously, check it out or carry it out. One time Mrs. Tweedie commented to me about a dream, connecting it with a suggestion for a new orientation for me. It kindled a strong process in me, two weeks of it. Turning over questions, restlessness, deliberation—until I came to the exact opposite of what Mrs. Tweedie had suggested. The essential thing here was the process that was kindled.

There are perhaps other shadow sides that I am unaware of at the moment. We are becoming more reflective, the awareness is changing and it's good to make it an issue and look again and again at it. Nothing is perfect in this world, also not the human being—that's impossible—otherwise, we wouldn't need to be living. When something is perfect, it simply dies. Life, however, is constant change. Only in this movement can God mirror Himself.

Ego Dissolution and the World of Appearance

There are so many concepts around that have to do with dying before you die, about the dissolving of the ego that, instead of making a new person of us in a certain way have a rather crippling effect. There are ideas of self-mortification that have nothing to do with the process of dissolving the ego. It took me a very long time to understand what it actually means, that the ego dissolves. Because I had images that were much too narrow. How can one understand this process and really bring it in relation to oneself?

For one thing, one has to understand that when it has to do with ego dissolution one needs to recognize being identified.

What does that mean?

It begins for example with our body. We think we *are* our body. Or we think we *are* our feelings. There are people who function like this: if they experience intense emotions, whether these are feelings of love or anger or whatever, then they have the feeling, ah, I'm alive. Others come more from thinking and believe, if I think a lot and come up with concepts, if I grasp a lot of connections intellectually, then I'm alive. I think, therefore I am. This is another way of being. There are many different perceptions along these lines.

We know today that there are no two identical perceptions, even when we speak of the same event. So *perception* is not objective, it doesn't offer any "security".

If we look inside ourselves, we gradually discover the ways in which we define ourselves as "I am this". I am a mother—this can offer a meaning in life—I'm a professor, I'm a doctor, I'm a cleaning woman, I'm the greatest, I'm nothing, I'm a mess, I can't do anything, I'm very creative, and so on. Everything which we identify ourselves as—if we think "I am this", as an individual—is identification. The best thing to begin with is to observe oneself. Wherever a strong attraction appears, there will probably also be strong attachment. Wherever one feels angry or enraged, where one's buttons get pushed or where a reaction of hurt comes, this is where one will be able to discover "being identified". In the process of disengaging, we gradually learn to understand, I am not this, I also cannot be that, and not that either. If I think that I'm the body and the body gets sick, then I have a problem. Who am I then, what is this "I"? This is the process of gradually peeling away the onion layers, in which we inwardly understand, it's true that I'm a mother and have this function, but one day the children will fly away, then I'm no longer primarily "mother". And when I die—what remains then?

We start to engage in the questions, where do I come from, where am I going. Or—as the Sufis so beautifully say it—with a ship that is sinking, what is left to me? We come from "I am a professor", "I am a mother" to *I am.* It is a condition of being. One can have a job, be a father, be a mother, but we are not *identified* with this function; instead we are rooted, we rest in this being that is Reality. Jesus said, I am the Way, the Truth, and the Life. When someone dies, when the life force has departed from the eye, then it doesn't see anymore—even if the organ of the eye is still intact. This life, this which lets us see, this is what is real. Everything that is transitory, everything that changes, cannot be Reality. We get gradually led toward this on the path. At first we are led into love, and then, if we are still able to name anything in this world, into "I am", this Life.

These images of dying before death, of mortification, of the-ego-must-go—these images don't just come from nothing. How does this process happen? You said that you could hardly cross a bridge in London one time, your situation was so existential, because you wanted to throw yourself off it.

Yes, that was a moment of extreme desperation. There are such moments. They can have a cathartic effect, be a milestone, but I also don't want to dramatize it too much—it can be, but doesn't have to be. It can also be that the process goes on quietly, without dramatic outer things happening. Inwardly yes, I think inwardly this enormous friction, this tension, does happen. But I see in all of it an organic process, how attachment is taken from us. The insight and the understanding are given, in the way we move into the empty space, into the Higher Self, on the Atmic level through the meditation and saying the mantra. The process happens organically.

We have "only" to endure.

We have to be awake. It has to happen consciously. And then comes the endurance. If we are not aware of what is happening, then it can easily go into unconsciousness again. So endure and observe, be aware, be awake. Guruji once said, we should be as alert as a cat in front of a mouse-hole. This is a great quality.

We watch the dreams, things that happen in the outside world, the hints we receive. When we get sick, we take this for instance as an opportunity to reflect on the transitory nature of the body. And in this way we come into a space where we say, ah, that's just something that simply *is*. Independent of whatever condition the body happens to be in at the moment. These are processes that gradually happen. I would never speak of mortification; I find that a medieval way to express it. It's a process—I think, too, that today it's easier, in a certain way. It may sound strange, but I'm sure that Mrs. Tweedie accomplished an enormous pioneering work with her life and through her book. People who are the first to live through this archetype, like Christ or Buddha, for example—they perform pioneer work; this is a tremendous effort. We "profit" from Mrs. Tweedie's work. We no longer have to do quite the same work. I also see this in the continuation of the generations, that I, for example, got to have another consciousness than my parents. And my children—they receive a great deal through my process of becoming aware. There is a development here.

The ego is not killed, the ego remains, but it finds its right place. It becomes a servant of the Higher Self. As long as we are unconscious, the ego reigns and we are its slaves. Naturally we need this egoic constellation, as long as we are in this world we don't go away from this mortal body. Only—it is just that we recognize that this body is a *relative* truth. It comes and goes, and with it also the feelings, thinking, perception, sensations. We put the ego in the right place. We need the power contained within it to actually live in this world. And this life is precious because only as a human being do we have the capacity to realize.

Now that would be the way in the sense of a development, in the image of the wheel defined as a spoke. But there's another way to look at it. This comes about when the human being has left the spoke and entered the spaceless space of the hub. This effects a paradigm change. Here, there is nothing to accomplish.

How difficult this ego dissolution is depends fully on the strength of one's own resistance. If we are nothing, then there's no problem. The more we're attached, the more we're identified with that which we are *not*, the more difficult the process will be, the more painful. It is a question of resistance, and this gets broken somewhere—more through the simple presence of the teacher than how he or she handles the disciple on the outside. Although that too plays a role, of course. Beloved executioner, Mrs. Tweedie would say about her teacher. It is really a mercilessly merciful path. It leads us steadily into nothing. It is the greatest liberation.

From the moment I entered into a relationship with Mrs. Tweedie, with the path, even though it was madness all around, *something* in me was only happy. And this, I think, everyone feels. Being identified also represents a kind of bondage; it is difficult in all respects to maintain all these things, these problems, these worries. Mrs. Tweedie said, 90 percent of all problems are made by oneself. This is true. It's an enormous liberation *and* it hurts. Yes, of course! But when I know that it hurts because it's my resistance and not because somebody wants something from me…

The inner pressure, like in this alchemical vessel, this is really present and can be immense. Whether a path is easy or hard, one can't really say. It's for sure always quite different than what one imagines. I can just say from my experience that it's the only worthwhile thing—because one becomes free, because one is at home with oneself and in everything. Something inside begins to celebrate, and this is actually the natural state.

Somewhere one has always longed for that, always had a perception of it even if it was hidden way in the background.

Always. Every person. Nature lets that happen herself. Every tree is celebrating, every bird sings praises. The sea, the wind, the clouds. Everything celebrates. The human being has to learn to do this. This is his very nature and his great sorrow if he cannot. This celebration is his natural state; it is not an ecstatic one. We do experience ecstatic states, experiences of unity—yes, the *unio mystica* does really happen. And then—I love this statement from Teresa of Avila: we are finally normal. It is something self-evident, something absolutely natural—we are finally human. Maybe later I shall say something more about what comes after enlightenment.

We live our lives exactly the same as before, we do what we have to do. What this fragrance, this color, this song have conveyed to us we sing or we do or we leave alone. It is quite simple. One says Yes to what is. Accepted. Surrenders to what is. Surrender is an important issue on this path; we already spoke about it. We surrender ourselves to IT. We simply accept this fragrance. This fragrance is nothing other than IT, which manifests in this world in order to become known. Nothing more happens.

I was a hidden treasure and wanted to be recognized; thus I created the world.

Hadith Qudsi

What is meant by "world of appearance"—and that the world of appearance is an illusion?

One can try looking at it like this: here is the Source, the Nameless. From this Nameless, out of this Source arose the creation, the manifestation, the world of appearances. It's the way that modern physics and astronomy explain the universe. From some kind of a nothing arose the big bang in which matter—which there actually isn't any of—formed, which expands into the bubble of our universe and at any time can contract again, so that again nothing would remain.

Another way to look at it would be the image of a spider who is spinning a thread; the thread is arising from the spider. The thread is not the spider but without the spider there wouldn't be a thread. And the thread can't exist by itself alone. One can see the creation like this, the form. Another image that can help us is the comparison to the shadow. A shadow only exists when a sun is there and an object—for example, a tree. This shadow has no life of its own; it is only present when the sun is there and this tree.

The Platonic allegory of the cave.

Exactly. The shadow has no life of its own—this is the important thing. We are like this shadow. Everything that has form and name is like this shadow. This shadow can do nothing out of itself. We can really do nothing out of ourselves. That which lets us breathe is the Source. Is Life. Is the will of God. The spider web cannot move on its own; it cannot make a net on its own. It's the spider that weaves the net. Everything that manifests was formed according to the Source, the will of the Source. And will return to it again. These are all only concepts that can help make understanding possible.

The world of appearance is transitory. It comes, it goes. And that which comes and goes cannot be us. This one cannot understand, only experience.

We have to learn to distinguish between that which is eternal, the Life in us that continues after death, what was there before death, and that which takes form, lives through space and time and returns, dissolves again. Truly, we are not the latter. Mrs. Tweedie told me that we Sufis "identify" with the Higher Self. The Higher Self is that Life in us, which is eternal. This is divine, this is THAT which is unnamable. Ignorance is getting it all mixed up. Most of the time it is a muddle for the person, where he doesn't really know what actually belongs to me, what am I. If we look at our lives sometime, from childhood until our present age, we have changed indescribably, constantly—well, who are we then, really?

If I look at the world of feelings, there are millions of feelings that constantly come to the surface and then disappear. Thoughts—where do they come from, where do they go? What can I depend on, which feeling, what am I really? This is the level of appearance. We learn on the path to understand how these things come and go, that Something IS in everything, which is unchangeable. It takes time, it really takes time until the heart receives glimpses and is able to integrate it. More than anything, integrating it takes time.

At the end of her book, Mrs. Tweedie wrote about the recognition of that which she really is. Being all-one. Al-lone. And then she said, this can now only be realized on deeper and deeper and deeper levels.

Sometime the heart will understand it, and then it must become ever more absorbed in it. This takes time. Because Life, Truth, the Unchangeable—most of the time it comes gradually. Gradually it penetrates the consciousness so that it becomes the pillar of support, the thing that carries Life. Reality becomes certainty. The world of appearance dances along, but the human being is no longer identified with it; the world of appearance is observed as something that arises and recedes like a wave. In the world of form there is up and down, day and night, good and evil, heavy and light. But IT rests in the depths, at the bottom of the sea, in the ocean.

Essence

There's this saying by Martin Buber that for mystics the word is burning on their tongues, but that when they want to talk, they can actually only stammer and stutter. I know that in a way it is a sphere about which one cannot speak. And yet it is important to speak. Often now the word "essence" has been used—what is this essence? And in the background is always the experience of oneness—what is it that fundamentally changes a person through the experience of oneness? What happens here?

As a matter of fact, it is difficult to speak about the *unio mystica.* It is a fundamental experience that is dormant in each person. It is something that escapes words. Perhaps on seam or at the crossing point, where we come from this ONE into the day-to-day consciousness again, at this threshold words are used. There, this basic experience that is unnamable can be named. Maybe one can illustrate this with light, which is not visible itself but when it falls through a colored glass, it pours itself into a form and color spectrum, and at this point where color appears, words are possible again. These words used to express the *unio mystica,* this basic experience, are always personally colored. Always in the language of the inner unique alchemy, of the cultural environment and of course also the language of the path which one has undertaken. The fundamental experience itself is beyond these things. In that respect—what can I say?

I can only say what is experienced at the threshold, there where the transition soul-person is. Here, one is caressed by a deep peace, a deep silence, a tender bliss. It is important that the person knows that what he is seeking can only be found within. That he understands there is nothing to accomplish, nothing to look for because that thing that the person looks for, is himself. To experience this is the *unio mystica.* Most of the time, I really don't know if I should talk about myself now or...I...and here I'm stuttering...because—is there an "I" that still experiences something at all? That's just it. There isn't anybody. There isn't anybody who can still experience. That's why Bhai Sahib said, who is enlightened? There isn't anybody who can be enlightened.

In general, we talk very little in our Sufi tradition about enlightenment. It is one step to "experience" it and another to practice it, to live it. In most cases it once again takes time until the person is completely seized to the depths by the experience, until the experience has sunk so deeply into the everyday consciousness that he or she is truly guided by the empty inner space—that this happens as a matter of course.

Somewhere one "experiences". Gazing inward, nothing is there. Looking outside—what am I not? One is dog and the flea that bites into the coat of the dog; one is tree, sky, human, dirt on the ground—what am I not? But that takes time—it isn't usual that this happens with one experience; it takes time until this finds its way into every cell, this awareness, this light or whatever one wants to call it. It takes time. These experiences one cannot induce; they are given.

There are great teachers who have had deep, fundamental experiences—for example, Ramana Maharshi who had this experience of enlightenment at sixteen. It took him thirty years to integrate this, to connect the two worlds with each other and also to grant the earthly world a suitable place in his life. The transformation of the heart, the birth of the human being takes time. At the beginning, the *unio mystica* is perhaps experienced as an all-one-ness, one is perhaps suddenly one with the sky, with the stars, or with human beings. The separation between I and you gets permeable. And one could say, the wave says, I am the ocean. When this experience gets deeper, there is a point at which a fundamental paradigm shift in one's view takes place. There, the ocean says, I am the wave. With this, time and space are pierced. At the same time, however, we live in time and space. But the view of inner and outer, of creator and creation takes shape in such a way that there is only the ONE left. Not two. The nothingness, which contains everything in itself. The person has faded out, been annihilated—become nothing. And everything reveals itself as it is, in the NOW.

These are steps. I'm going to return once more to my personal experience. There was a time in which I had such inner experiences—with caution, I'd like to say this again—with this feeling, the wave becomes the ocean. I came back into my everyday consciousness and experienced myself as a person again. And I was actually dissatisfied; I had the idea that from then on there wasn't going to be a person anymore. But I still felt like a person, although at the same time this other mode of seeing slowly began to unfold, singing in my heart. Then, through some outer circumstances—I'll talk about them in a while—I came into great inner distress and knew that, now, in everyday life it was of central importance that IT transform this "I am Annette", I am this person. I prayed and struggled with this a lot, and then the Advaita teachings, the way Nisargadatta Maharaj formulated them in his writings *I am That,* helped me very much. As I later discovered, this aspect of Not-Two is also included in Mrs. Tweedie's book. Only in very few sentences—the time had not yet been ripe for it. There I really found the thread, as Guruji said, love and trust become one and that also passes and nothing remains but Nothingness. Because in the experience of *unio mystica*—if it can be grasped in words—when we refer to the bliss, the peace, the silence that we experience in it, we are still held within the love affair. Guruji directs us farther, he leads us farther, to that place where there is simply nothing more to hold on to. The ego can quite easily identify with this state of bliss, this state of "I am", of *ananda.* Guruji's statements lead us farther, to where one is simply nothing, cannot say anything, doesn't know. What is left to us, is, in the now, in the moment, to be present. That is all. Like Mechthild of Magdeburg says, one is like this leaf in the wind or this feather in the wind, or, like Mrs. Tweedie implied more from the human side, the feet find no place more on the earth to rest.

The path is actually a remedy, a cure; the meditation and the mantra are medicine for people, to return to themselves, to become healed and whole. It is possible that this medicine may one day no longer be needed; that is something everyone has to know for him or herself. We leave the boat and at the other shore we don't carry it with us any longer. We lay it down. Of course there remains in the heart this enormous gratitude and respect for this boat that has carried us, for this signpost Home. Of course this process is never finished. From our human point of view, we live within time and space. We are on the earth to learn, and to realize the learning. And these belong together. With "realize" I mean to bring it into the everyday. The process of absorption never ends. On the one hand, one can say one has arrived—and as so often we can only express things paradoxically—on another level this process is never-ending. Because if we were perfect, we would, as we said, die.

The everyday moves onward. We have duties, responsibilities. So we live on in this world, we are still subject to the principle of duality. Now one is healthy, now one is perhaps sick. Sometimes there's this, sometimes there's that, but more and more it is possible to simply perceive this occurrence as observer, as witness. It's as if the mantra swings us into a rhythm with the inner golden thread. The thread of the Eternal. The Essential in us rests in this placeless place, in the Higher Self, the empty space, and the deeper the "anchoring" in this empty space, the attention resting there, the more it is possible for us to be witness to what is, when we look outside. When we look inside, silence is there. There, too, thoughts sometimes come; dreams sometimes come in the night. Suddenly a shadow shows up again, suddenly there's a certain confrontation, a dispute with this world. One learns to simply look at these things. With time, one also has had a certain amount of practice in this. One looks at the things, well-acquainted.

One lets go of what goes on outside, returns to this center, to this empty space that is simply present. It just stabilizes itself there more and more. It takes time.

My experience is that the demands get bigger and bigger. The areas of friction become more acute and one is tested to see if even in extreme situations one can still be singing HIS song in one's heart.

There is nothing but Nothingness; this is the essence of our path.

Transmission of the Flame

Now I have another question about your work. In Mrs. Tweedie's book, it is only described how she gets indications from Bhai Sahib and then gradually and incidentally we find out that she should take over his work, be his successor. Over a long period of time you yourself were quietly prepared by Mrs. Tweedie for this task. Can you say more about this?

At first, my experience at that time, as I have said, was the biggest surprise to myself. It was a breakthrough. I can't call it anything else. Something broke through. I knew for years that something was coming. I never, ever knew what. And I must also say, I *never* had a thought in this direction—to take over this work. Not one. And so at first it was just a deep jolt, this breakthrough that came out of the blue. After the yes, yes, yes, from Mrs. Tweedie I experienced simply a great support from her, support of a very practical nature. I could ask her everything concerning other people when I wasn't sure, and also regarding my own further development. I always wrote to her, asked her everything, I didn't make one move without asking her. If I received an answer then it was clear. If I didn't receive one, then I went according to my inner voice. She was just accompanying me. In this sense, there wasn't so much to talk about because it felt so natural. For me it was like being a fish in the water, for the first time in my life. Mrs. Tweedie simply affirmed it. Sometimes she commented on something when I directed a seminar so that I got feedback. Or she gave me certain pointers, or she told me how people were to be handled, how I should deal with certain things, where I should pay attention. In this way the preparation took place.

Like a kind of training.

Yes. With the Buddhists it's the same way. At first, for example, a Zen student will receive permission to teach and acquires with it the title of *sensei.* After several years of teaching, if she has passed the "test period", she can be named *roshi.* With this, she accepts the work of carrying forward this Buddhist lineage. I see that I had a similar training period. I received assignments; Mrs. Tweedie watched how I did it—whether it was right or whether it was not right. Once I received a letter from her in which she criticized me and reprimanded me. It was like a thunderclap for me. It is not that I didn't do my best and didn't really try to be alert. However, it is true that the blind spot is just the blind spot that one doesn't see. This letter plummeted me into an enormous inner distress. I already talked about the time when I encountered the Advaita teachings—it had to do with completely overcoming the "person". That was really a struggle, also for help. Because I longed for nothing more than to leave everything behind me. But one cannot *do* it. And I accepted her letter immediately, everything that she said. She was deeply interested in seeing how I would react. I tried with all my might to dissolve it; of course it was the ego, these were ego problems. I tried and tried and then came to a point where I thought, I can't work like this anymore. I was ready to give up the function of teaching. The conditions had become unbearable; I got sick and inwardly I shrivelled.

I went to Mrs. Tweedie in this situation. At this meeting she authorized me, "in full consent" to carry on the tradition of the Naqshbandiyya Mujaddidiyya Sufi lineage. And then she said, "Carry it on wherever you want and however you want." She said, "...if you want." There is always free will. Always freedom. And what else would one want to do, Anna, you know?

I will always do it. Whether with people who come to me or without, that doesn't play a role at all. When one has made oneself available and does this work—then there's nothing else to do. Many think it must be fantastic and wonderful. But one can't imagine what suffering one has to put up with in such work and what happens in the way of psychic pressure. Mrs. Tweedie said, one needs broad shoulders. She was quite modest. Just said, one needs broad shoulders. One sees everything, endures everything, my goodness...but this is only a small part. This is incidental, really.

You had nine years with Mrs. Tweedie by your side for this process. Now it's been one year since Mrs. Tweedie died. Has anything changed because of that for you?

Yes. During those nine years I just listened very, very carefully to what Mrs. Tweedie would say. My attention was actually there all the time. With her death, the attention was thrown back to my own core. That did change. It's also true that a certain further development happens. It wasn't possible for me as long as Mrs. Tweedie was still living because I knew how precious the remaining time was. She was 92 years old. One knows that there is not much time left, so all my attention was really directed to her. Now I cannot ask her anymore in *this* way—that is really different—there's no longer a person, someone sitting opposite in a physical sense, with whom one can speak, whom one gets to ask. That is a great change. Something has been taken, but at the same time something has been given. And now it has become possible that the perfume, the specific color—not the essence—slowly merges with the environment. This is a process that happens slowly. Sometimes I have to summon up courage to stand by *this* perfume in this way, to allow it to happen. Mrs. Tweedie, Bhai Sahib, Guru Maharaj—these are great models. Who am I? I don't know. And so one does what one has to do. I just try to do what needs to be done. That's all. Not less.

By the way, transmission is *always* one of the most difficult things that there is about a tradition—the handing over from one to another. This is very delicate. We can also see this with other schools, or teachers, with Karmapa, Kirpal Singh, Muktananda, Ayya Khema. This is quite a difficult matter. Mrs. Tweedie told me at the very end that Guruji never spoke about transmission. It's also interesting that this word is not to be found in Mrs. Tweedie's book. She was never expressly appointed as successor. And she told me that Guruji just appointed the most capable people. That he did do, but he did *not* speak of transmission.

Really—the teacher has no name, no face; it is not a question of a person, not a matter of a name or a specific face. It is a question of THAT, which has no form, no name. Being present. This is the only thing that has an effect. The empty space. I think it is really important to understand this. If we identify with a person, then maybe this can be necessary for a time, but in the final analysis it is about no name, no face, no form, no way. Only about THAT. This is also a process of becoming mature. Like relating to the idea of God. Every religion says, don't create images of God for yourself. And what happens? Here, too, mature understanding is needed—there is nothing other than IT. THAT.

Inquiry

A*nnette, before we come to an end, I would like to inquire again about several points more closely. For example, you said that in connection with the journey in God, that this is the next step as far as development goes, which will find a language. As I spoke about destroying the ego, you had the opinion that this is medieval language. It appears that mysticism in our time does not have a really up-to-date language. I found it very exciting, for example, when I heard from Dorothee Soelle, "Mysticism needs to be made democratic"—suddenly in this sentence, centuries and totally different realms are meeting. For me it had a really refreshing effect. Willigis Jaeger thinks that modern natural science will deliver the images and concepts to mystical spirituality, with which it will be able to articulate itself. How do you see this? How do you yourself experience this in your work? Do you feel a shortcoming here?*

As a matter of fact, there is a difficulty. It almost seems like language is shedding its skin.

On the one side, mystics have found a language in poetry that we understand, that is almost timeless, like the Japanese haikus or Rumi's poems. This language has a timeless dimension. But if we have to explain a path and instead of speaking in poetic words, in hints and analogies we have to speak in a linear way, then we are lacking a language for this. We've also felt this sometimes in our conversation together. We still have many old images, out of the Bible for example, that have imprinted on our minds, which somehow still carry us. I think that what we have to do today is to let go of whatever is ballast or superfluous in order to develop an everyday language, a mystical everyday language that has a certain matter-of-factness about it, not something put on or sanctimonious.

M*aybe a language with which one can simply relate what one actually does, without it sounding strange or embarassing. A language with which one can also communicate to one's mother or colleague what group one goes to on Thursday evening.*

Yes. This is of course conditioned by society, by our values, by our inner orientation and by our picture of the world that leaves little room for a different understanding. The natural sciences teach us today that the picture of the world that we come from is actually medieval and that the basic orientation how we see the world no longer holds up with the newest findings. So there is a lot on the move in terms of openness and new orientations. In this process, language too will probably become more everyday, or it will find a place that will be more matter-of-fact and everyday.

This openness surely reaches far beyond language.

Of course. When, for example, the Buddhist teacher Ani Tenzin Palmo advocates in her video "The Nature of the Mind" that today the human being just doesn't need to know everything, for example, what the 38 aspects of the mind are. That it is just not that important anymore. That actually a person only has to know what kind of effect the mind has on him and how he should deal with it. The old training in Tibetan Buddhism still demanded of one to memorize these 38 aspects. That takes an incredible amount of time and requires strong concentration until one has the whole training behind one. And I think that today much will be scaled off, so to speak, so that it's no longer necessary to know all these things.

Perhaps because we are in a culture that is inundated with knowledge—and spirituality brings us simplicity once again.

We have to go straight for the core. This of course requires a certain courage on the part of the teacher to find a language which can let go of much of the respective tradition and really push forward to the core teaching. A language that every normal person can understand and fathom. After all, to realize oneself is the most natural thing in the world; it is inherent in each person. One doesn't have to go to church or practice this or that ritual or memorize some kind of creed to do it. The new language will arise from the core.

The natural sciences are absolutely forcing us to this, they'll simply pull the rug out from under us with our usual picture of the world. In this way something new begins.

Bernie Glassman, for example, compiled koans with different people, koans that are no longer Buddhist but instead can be understood by people of all cultures. This is interesting. You see, there are different people in different schools who involve themselves with this process of exposing the core of the teachings as precisely and simply as possible. There the dialogue will take place, there lies the regeneration.

A further aspect is that people today know more and more themselves what speaks to them. That is one thing. On the other hand, there is of course the need for the mirror from outside; this is still helpful. These emancipating steps in the spiritual realm are really a walk along the edge. "To make mysticism democratic"—this has to do with the fact that the human being is responsible for himself in the scope of spirituality too. And on the other hand, it's necessary to allow guidance in where he doesn't see for himself. This is delicate because of course the ego can sneak in everywhere.

But in general, the tendency moves in this direction. We talk more about spirituality; we have more access to the basic esoteric knowledge of different paths. There are more and more books about this, which means that people are interested, they are slowly forming a picture. Previously, this was not at all possible. In this way one comes of age sooner, can recognize earlier what is necessary for oneself. If one is really true and earnest—and this is the essential—every path leads Home. If one is profoundly aligned toward the ONE, it is automatically like this.

All paths are accessible to us through this opening of the ways and you just said again that every way leads us to the Truth. But how is it if the paths mix? Zen and Christian mysticism can, for example, support each other; but how is it if I take a little from here and a little from there, if I switch around all the time, path-hopping or spiritual shopping—mustn't one still stay consistently on one spoke today in order to reach the goal?

From my experience I have to quite clearly affirm that. I have been able to observe that most of the time it has not brought people much who change very often. One comes up against one's own edges through the practice on one path; one arrives at certain points. And exactly at this point one frequently changes paths; one thinks, no, this is not so good after all, no, this or that teacher isn't it, either. And they try the next one. Then it works out again for a while until one again reaches this point. To realize oneself means to cross over this points. to perceive one's own limitations, step through and go on. If one changes too often, this maturing, this fermenting process cannot really happen. One can only accompany someone on the path if there is a certain continuity.

If, for example, someone comes to me and actually practices Zen, is maybe there just one time and then has some types of experiences, it's quite difficult for me to speak about them with this person.

Why?

I know the training on this one spoke, I know the dynamic in it, the steps, the secret pathways, the difficulties. About these things I can speak. If one changes often, one can't say anything at all.

That's the one point. My personal experience is that one should scrutinize the paths, choose one and then truly walk it.

But it can be that the person inwardly bumps up against something at a particular point in time, and then it's very possible that one either sends him to someone else or recommends to him a practice that one knows from another path.

***For** a particular point?*

For a particular point or a particular situation. I've related to you my experience with the teaching of Nisargadatta Maharaj. Or the story that Mrs. Tweedie always told us, how she dreamed about a particular place in Maghreb: when she had finally found this place and the teacher, she was sent away again after a short time. Every path has its emphasis, its definite strength in the training. It can happen that a situation comes about where a very particular inner aspect will be brought to a person's attention that needs work; for example, mindfulness. Then perhaps for a period of time the mantra will not stand in the foreground but the practice of mindfulness instead. Even though mindfulness training is naturally included in our path, it isn't so deliberately taught as, for example, in Buddhism. I mean it in this way.

I've also understood over the course of time that meditation is not *the* vehicle for every person. For the one person, this may be right, for another, that—so I can't say, absolutely, this is for *all* people. This is not possible. I also can't say, only this path takes you Home. I just can't say this. I know that it's not right. At any rate, I can only work with the experiences on the Path in which I've been trained. This is my tool.

***More** than once during the course of our conversation you've said that the work on oneself goes on for one's whole life and that even after integrating mystical experiences, shadow parts will be in us for life. That implies the question for me: won't one ever be rid of one's structure?*

At first, we just get to know ourselves. Then this experience is given—quietly or quite deeply, sometimes shockingly—the experience of love, of oneness, of nothingness. Going through such a deep mystical experience, which we've said can be quite subtle, hardly tangible but sometimes also dramatic like a blow one is dealt doesn't mean that we stay in this state. In nine out of ten cases the experience of oneness does not mean that the ego structure is totally transformed. I already mentioned Ramana Maharshi, who had this deep experience at sixteen and then needed many years to integrate it, to connect the two worlds to each other again.

The question is how radical the mystical experiences are, whether the ego structure really gets transformed through them. For many people this is a process that is certainly not settled with one single experience. This issue is being raised actually only recently. A so-called enlightenment experience doesn't guarantee that the ego disappears.

This also has to do with what we just talked about—that there is still little language available for this domain, for this living-*in*-God. Today we have different teachers who have had such experiences and realize that for example they can still be hurt, that they themselves offend. It's beginning to be talked about. Actually, until now the mystical paths were defined up to the point of enlightenment. Most of the stories in Zen, for example, end with "...and he was enlightened." But how it looks afterward, very little is said about this. Today an exchange is beginning on this subject, simply because one notices—hey, there's still this person; what's supposed to happen now, what's the next step?

E*verybody has issues that partly begin very early on through conditioning, through the culture or the stamp with which one generally came here into the world. I have the impression that something of this always remains. Also after experiences, after integrating the experiences. You said that the shadow realms never totally dissolve. Something of the edge, of the peculiarities of a person just remains, even after all the experiences and all the integration of these experiences.*

What you say is right. We did come to this earth with a particular fragrance. "Fragrance" is always an aspect of the uniqueness of the person. One could also say "note". A "C" is a "C", a "G" is a "G", "minor" is "minor". And in that, a certain structure remains. One doesn't have to put a value on them, whether they're good or bad. But this note, this color, this fragrance, it survives. Because IT is reflected in the multiplicity. The ONE mirrors itself in these billions of aspects of the ONE. Since we *have* to live this fragrance, this color, this uniqueness, it remains with us. If we are, for example, sanguine types, we won't suddenly become phlegmatic, or the other way around. The sanguine temperament will continue, basta. This is part of the fragrance, of the sound—this continues. The difference is that one can simply observe it: ah, when it comes to temperament, IT wants to express itself in a sanguine way. This is HIS expression; one isn't identified but sees that it's the dance of Maya, the dance of the appearances. One is like a witness, who observes. It will always be like this.

When we talk about the shadow that we need to integrate, I don't take this to be the most difficult kind of work. The first time I heard the words "shadow work", I cringed because I thought, uh-oh. I was overwhelmed and thought I could never manage that. Today I have a kind of love relationship to the shadow. It's there—so what? I greet it, look at it, and continue. That's all. So it's not so heavy. It belongs to life like doing the dishes. Everything has its place, doesn't have a value put on it.

This aspect, that enlightenment doesn't yet mean integration—let's talk about this a little more specifically. Mrs. Tweedie's book ends also with her describing her experience of oneness by way of intimation. A short time before, her teacher had said to her that she—after everything she had undergone—was still nowhere, and that this was just the beginning of the spiritual path. So—how does it continue, actually? After enlightenment.

I always have to secretly laugh when I hear "enlightenment". So many images are mixed up in this.

There is this inner experience that everything is one and that what we are is in reality nothing. In essence. This can be an experience that lasts a second, a half a second. It can also be more lasting. Most people fall out of it again and come back into this world. Then one is confronted with oneself again, one experiences conflicts, friction, feels hurt, and still presumably offends others as well.

This is first of all to be fundamentally accepted. "Enlightened person"—what does this actually mean? There are so many ideas connected to this. I believe that when one goes through these processes oneself, one gets quieter. One notices when one is sincere, truthful with oneself, how this deep experience can play into the everyday and also how it can let one fall into duality. The point is to admit to it. Purely and simply. Of course it's true that these states of oneness deepen when one continues to practice. It becomes more and more an inner certainty; something which was only very delicate before, perhaps like a silvery tinkling of a bell suddenly becomes a deep-sounding gong that resounds for a long, long time. This condition allows us to linger in a sense of being that is impersonal. There is simply an awareness there, without being personally involved, without being irritated by the change of appearances. My experience is that these periods that at first are little sequences extend themselves in time. Then they disappear again. Then they come again. A certain effort is still needed in the sense of being aligned.

I can't claim that I am always in a state of oneness. I notice sooner when I'm outside and I can bring myself more quickly back into this Being again. When one can give this Being, this divine state, just *one* quality at all, then it is love. This on the one hand deepens and on the other hand extends itself in time. But it takes much, much time.

It demands the willingness to look at all the areas that one hasn't yet integrated in the everyday—to look at them, to allow them, to become reconciled with them, to say Yes. And everyday life will show us that life is the greatest teacher. There are people who have had enlightenment experiences, were for a long time in a monastery, have a keen mind but when, for example, they return to normal life are totally underdeveloped, emotionally.

Perhaps it's necessary to work on one's emotional parts for further growth. Who knows. One will feel it inwardly, everyone can find it out for him or herself. I think it is a question of a spiral process. Today, different teachers from the West and the East are aware that great enlightenment experiences don't necessarily guarantee that the ego is no longer there. This means to be alert, to continue to learn. There is a beautiful Indian wisdom saying that goes like this:

The world is illusion,
everything is Brahman,
the world is Brahman.

We don't need to talk much about the first sentence, *the world is illusion. Everything is Brahman* is this experience of oneness or the experience of nothingness in which we know we aren't this, we aren't that, so that this experience of enlightenment is actually an ex-clusive one. Now there's the third sentence—*the world is Brahman.* This means you are Brahman, the tree is Brahman, the blackbird out there is Brahman, the guy who is making me mad is Brahman, the hunger in Africa is Brahman—and this is something that one could call an almost in-clusive enlightenment experience, which embraces everything and makes no distinctions. I mean all of this not in an intellectual sense, but lived. Real. This is of course a large proposition and it demands time. In this way we need to translate this inner experience of enlightenment quite practically. Because of this, too, our path is a way of life. In this lies a real greatness.

I'm convinced that we have our whole life for it. It doesn't matter whether we have "attained" integration by the end of our life or whether we haven't "attained" it. We are simply people, and inside is the certainty that everything is nothing.

In this way I can look quite practically at my days, my failures, my weaknesses, and I don't judge myself for them. I look and say okay. The more this peeling back of the personality happens there is certainly more and more a lightness in all of it. It happens and it's also like a gift to one as well.

This Being for me possesses a heart quality, it's so endlessly wide and open. One is simply awake, that's the state of being. And the more IT is allowed to be, the more spontaneous and natural life becomes. I don't have to make efforts to achieve something, there isn't anything to achieve. One simply observes HIS reflection. Then everything receives a certain lightness, an ease. More and more. Guruji did say, at the beginning the path is strenuous and then it gets easier. It definitely gets easy.

But it's certainly not a straight line from A to B, and the line doesn't go steadily upward. Sometimes there are assaults of despair—like not from this world. But when one knows this and there too goes more into an observing mode, one can accept more and more that it's just part of it.

Maybe this aspect has something to do with the fact that so many people are afraid of the Path. I always see that peoples' eyes are full of longing, that they gobble up the literature and the books, that they know where the nearest meditation group is meeting—but they don't go. What is your experience, people come to you "new"—what do you think this fear is about? This hesitation to take the step and to enter the Path.

These can be very different reasons. I think for sure that one is the fear of losing so-called control over one's life. People are really convinced that they've got life in their grasp. Of course if you look closely it's not like that. But here is certainly a place where fear crystallizes.

Ah, fears are so various. There's also the fear of being confronted with yourself—one is simply afraid of oneself. One is afraid of being seduced or mislead; one has heard of sects, of abuse in the spiritual domain.

I think there is a kind of sense in people that something in life could radically change and a part of our being is afraid, it twists and turns away from this. These fears don't just manifest in the spiritual domain, they are also reflected in other areas of life. This is the fear of change—actually the fear of death and along with that the fear of life.

One feels all of this before, probably. Somewhere one knows that he will be confronted with very deep questions. There is this quiet presentiment there.

That it gets easier, or serene or as you have said that one feels a kind of being held in the dark times—one doesn't have a feeling for any of this; this is still closed to one in this phase of approaching the Path. I think it would be lovely, Annette, if, after all that we've mentioned about phases and stages, you could once again make clear—as far as one can describe it at all, in words—what a joy it is, or how this life is when it is easy. I won't ask you, wasn't it fun to have gone on a spiritual path.

That'd be a bit over the top.

Yes, that would be over the top. Although the question about fun does belong in our time.

Of course. Let's say it'd be kind of a challenging question.

Well, you talked about how you've worked on yourself, what you gave up and went through—what for? Where is actually the fun here now?

Where is the fun here? You know, humor, fun, lightness come about when you can just see as this whole being. And when you see how you exert yourself, how you take this seriously and that seriously. And suddenly, from the role of observer, you find that unbelievably funny. What a crawling, what a scratching, what a shoveling! Well, when I can succeed in keeping this perspective, and this happens more and more, then I have to just smile. I look at everything as if I were sitting in the theater. We do go to the movies, to the theater to amuse ourselves, to have fun, and watch all these comedies and dramas. We think the plays of Shakespeare are fantastic and pay a lot of money—and actually it's playing the whole time in our lives, we just have to take this step back from ourselves, be a witness, be present. Then sometimes it gets really funny. It's unbelievable if one looks at everything like this. And then—maybe fun isn't the right word—then it gets light, one laughs at oneself, sometimes also at others. And this perspective gives you a certain lightness. Spiritual way and fun—you know, I've also suffered in my life, I've talked about it, and at some point I wanted to be a little freer and to suffer a bit less, and I just looked around to see what kinds of gateways there might be. Spiritual life held the promise for me that it gets easier and that one could overcome suffering.

At the beginning it was certainly difficult, but it did really become easier and easier. Although seen from the outside, life itself doesn't get easier—it's not like that. If it is gifted to one, to be able to fall more and more out of personal identification, then it gets lighter. And you know, to meditate, for example, is just not strenuous for me. At the very beginning, meditating or the *dhikr* or each practice was hard at first, but very quickly it gets easier. When I meditate, I'm at the Source, this is soul nourishment for me, this is relaxation and restoration for me, like when a balled-up piece of tissue paper slowly unfolds itself again or like a poppy, whose wrinkled petals slowly become smooth in their opening. This is what meditation is for me. This is not a strain. Saying the *dhikr* is tuning in to eternity—how can that be an effort?

Normal Human Being

***How** does your life look today?*

In the meantime, both of my children are out of the house. They are grown. When the children were still small, I naturally wondered, what should I do with them, should I teach them meditation or a mantra or what should I do. But we leave the children alone on our path. Mrs. Tweedie told us that the parents take the children with them by way of their being. It is truly like this, that a yogi changes the world through his being. And, Mrs. Tweedie added with a smirk, it's the most subversive way to change the world. I, of course, really liked hearing that....

I still teach t'ai chi, have a t'ai chi school; I earn my living mainly with this.

Recently added to this is the *Villa Unspunnen,* a wonderful place, by the way, that in a way really looked for us too. This place is full of silence, a place of discovery. I see it as a vessel. The heart of this place is absolute silence for me, nothingness, this is the invisible ground. This vessel that is at our disposal should on the one hand serve the people who follow the Sufi path—meditation takes place here twice a week—and then for retreats, seminars, and for the silent times. On the other hand, I would like to give other mystical paths, teachers from other traditions who are no strangers to this deep empty space the opportunity to carry out their teachings and meditations here. So that slowly, star-shaped, maybe an exchange results out of which something new develops, a universal spirituality, perhaps. I see the place as a luminous point that should inspire and serve people who really want to learn actively. It's very important to me also that we try to "walk our talk" here. To live what we have realized, and that also means to share it, also in a material sense. We've established an association "Open Hands", with which we support projects in different developing countries and the project "A smile a day for one world".

In addition to this, we also have the silent times at *Windschnur* in Bavaria and talks and seminars in Germany and Switzerland, so I have a pretty full day-to-day life.

I live with my husband. Of course I continue to practice, when it calls me. My whole life is dedicated to the ONE. I do what I have to do, let go of what I have to let go. I get up in the morning, meditate, have breakfast and then work time begins with preparing talks, with correspondence, business meetings, talks with people who have personal or spiritual problems. Most of the time I try to take a daily walk, do t'ai chi—in other words, to have some breathing room between the everyday work. In the evening I usually meditate once again, sometimes I watch an informative program on television or I read. Before going to sleep I collect myself again very consciously. Often I'm on the road giving talks, seminars or at Windschnur. Once a year I withdraw completely, travel somewhere in order to be quite alone with the ONE.

Wherever I am, whatever I do—I try at each moment to be in HIS presence, to be present. I follow the voice of the heart. Fullness has room there, the fullness of life, we don't exclude anything. Withdrawal also has room in this. In a way, the connection of both worlds really happens in the everyday. The way I experienced so clearly during the first visit with Mrs. Tweedie in London, as I entered her home.

Mrs. Tweedie frequently quoted this sentence: "Love and do what you want." t's a sentence from Saint Augustine. We simply ARE. There aren't any particular virtues or a particular way that we *should* live. Of course there are ethical guideposts, like for example the *ahimsa* principle—not to kill—which in our tradition is very radically understood. It is not just about not killing other living beings but in the end also about not hurting the feelings of others and oneself. In this sense, for example, the habit of drinking coffee every day is already an injury. Because then the person is no longer free. Whereas earlier I felt these ethical guidelines to be coming from outside, today with the introduction into one's own essence, the doing happens by itself, quite naturally and spontaneously. *What* I do is not so decisive, it is the *how*. Doing is natural and spontaneous, not because the principle is so internalized but because IT is functioning out of itself. It is the principle of creation that is set free.

There is no "should" and "must". This should and must is very often related to conditioning that we have experienced through the family or the society or through ourselves; this puts its stamp on us and often covers over this principle of creation, the very nature of our being. We live in a way quite naturally—whatever that may mean—our Being. We *are*.

Let me return once more to this picture of the wheel. The spoke is the *path of love* upon which we have been guided and led, and then there is this change where we come into the hub, where we leave everything behind. Maybe I can give you an example for this. One instructs someone about how to cook vegetables. At the beginning one says, ok, now you turn on the stove, then you take a frying pan, some oil and onions, and then the vegetables. After maybe ten minutes one gives the instruction to turn off the stove again. That can appear contradictory, of course—one time it's "turn it on", another time it's "turn it off". In the meantime, the process of getting cooked is carried out. We need certain bridges or crutches or supports, which at a given time are then set aside or dissolved again.

This is also a way to explain that instructions to students can turn out quite differently, although the question may have been exactly the same one. The point is to see exactly where a person is standing. For example, the image of a raging river appears in a dream. In one situation, the "instruction" will be: throw yourself in. To another person, who may be in a very fragmented phase at the moment, the appropriate thing to do is to stand at the shore, to really stand there and to concern oneself about structure. It is always the question of level. It is important to grasp exactly where the person stands. And the answer aims right there. Of course another aspect is that people are different by nature. The one needs more strictness; to him one says for example, more or less directly: meditate more. Another practices too strenuously and needs to be more relaxed.

As I've already mentioned, much is communicated on the path of love about one's own experiences. It's true that book knowledge can be helpful but it's knowledge acquired from outside. If I read a book about skiing, that doesn't mean I can ski. But if I stand up on the skis and make the first attempts, I get a taste of what it really means to ski. In this sense, experiences are given to us on the path. And there, on the threshold to the hub, we have to also leave the experiences behind. That is to say, they are left behind. There is the danger—and this is also why a teacher is important—that the ego settles in and begins to identify with the mystical experience. This is the danger of inflation, as it's called in psychology. A watchful eye is needed here, also of course for oneself. But as a matter of fact, in essence, we leave the mystical experiences behind because there is nobody there who can experience. IT is experiencing itself. IT is recognizing itself through the reflection, becomes aware of itself. HE had longed to be recognized, longed for His treasure, His treasures to be recognized.

There is actually only *experience,* not *I experience,* but rather *IT* experiences itself. The I is the veil and it is lifted.

Many get stuck in the spoke. If one is caught there, the danger of dogmatism exists. The Dalai Lama made a wonderful statement when he said, the deeper the realization, the smaller appear the differences. He meant this in relation to the different traditions. And this is really like that.

I see myself as universal spirit. This has more to do with the time into which I was born than with my personality. One is simply born and is unique. This is IT. Every person is IT. Pure IT.

In each tradition we meet the original universal spirit and every tradition has its particular light ray as part of the whole. In Buddhism, the Bodhisattva ideal touches me especially. When we look at Mrs. Tweedie, this love that she felt for each individual person—this is Bodhisattva quality for me. We learn this too on the path. We learn to see a person, to look through his persona and to see the heart. And when one sees the heart, endless love simply flows. One understand this person from one's deepest heart. The Bodhisattva quality is something that really connects me to Buddhism, this taking part in the world of appearances, compassion. Compassion has two qualities. The one is that we feel the vulnerability of the other, what concerns him as body, as form, as face and name. One grieves and suffers with him. The second component of compassion is that the person sees this light in the other, this light that is eternal. And this fills with the greatest joy. These two components make it possible to feel what is in the Other.

In Islam I feel the metaphysical to be the most developed compared to other traditions. This *La illaha ill'allah* is the central pole, the declaration that there is nothing but God. This is a pillar that lies centrally hidden in every religion, but Islam is unique in its clear expression. It is this statement that once lead the Sufis to go there and which Bhai Sahib opened so endlessly wide with his "There is nothing but Nothingness." The other is the principle of surrender.

All traditions speak of love—this is the greatest power in the whole universe. It can move mountains, it is the highest dynamic. If we speak of a universal consciousness or universal spirit, I can now of course only address small parts. In Hinduism it is the Advaita teaching which becomes absorbed in the Not Two that touches me particularly deeply. In the last two or three years of her life, Mrs. Tweedie mentioned again and again that if she could give talks again, she would talk about the Bhagavadgita. She had actually planned, two years before her death, to drum up a kind of study group that would study the Bhagavadgita. The Bhagavadgita can be a great help on the way of transformation; it deepens the understanding that there is no doer, that the human being can live in a manner that leaves no traces. The central point is that the person does not identify with himself as a separate doer. This helped me enormously. And this does in fact connect in a certain way to our tradition. In Bhai Sahib's company, the Ramayana was often read aloud, the Vedas were quoted; we are in the tradition of the Indian Naqshbandiyya Mujaddidiyya lineage.

I feel drawn to the Christian mystics through their language, which corresponds to my cultural background. They inspire me because they speak the same inner language as I. I really like the fact that all mystics somehow speak the same language. The truth is one. And that resounds in the statements of Meister Eckhart, Hildegard von Bingen, Mechthild von Magdeburg, Madame de Guyon. For me they are a deep source of inspiration.

The language in Taoism, in the *Tao te Ching,* seems so wide and undogmatic, it leaves the person free and in certain things is extremely precise. The concept "the Unnamable" originates from the *Tao te Ching.* The Tao cannot be named. A glorious inspiration! The nature images in Taoism are also wonderful symbols. For example, the image of water that is able to split open a stone—that the soft can dissolve the hard, can change it, the water that flows in the deepest channels, which means on a symbolic level the deep channels of society, of people, its shadow sides. There, where nobody wants to go. These are just some examples from Taoism that move and inspire me.

This universal spirit I find also in our path. It is clear, simple, precise and at the same time wide as the sky. Form and emptiness permeate one other, the essence remains essence, this is the universal. Also, that everything is practiced in silence. If we can really say anything about the *unio mystica,* then we can actually only be silent. It is the silence that is able to reveal. And silence is common to every tradition. Every tradition leads to this absolute stillness, where the human being is quiet. Listens. And is absorbed. The self is left behind.

If you would like to contact Annette Kaiser, please write to the following address:

Annette Kaiser
Oberdorfweg 7
CH-3812 Wilderswil

If you would like information about events with Annette Kaiser in Switzerland and in Germany and/or the program of *Villa Unspunnen* and/or *Windschnur*, please contact:

Villa Unspunnen
Ch-3812 Wilderswil
Tel. 0041 (0) 33 821 04 44
Fax 0041 (0) 33 821 04 45
E-mail info@villaunspunnen.ch
www.villaunspunnen.ch

die windschnur
Windschnur 6—12
D-83132 Pittenhart

Tel. 0049—(0)8624—891 504
Fax 0049—(0)8624—891 508
E-mail info@windschnur.de
www.windschnur.de

Notes

FOREWORD

1. *The Chasm of Fire,* 1979, Element Books, Tisbury, Wiltshire, England; *Daughter of Fire,* 1986, Blue Dolphin Publishing, Nevada City, CA.

CHAPTER 1: THE SEARCH

1. From the magazine *Sufi,* No. 39, London, 1998, 19
2. Teresa of Avila, *Ich bin ein Weib—und obendrein kein gutes, (*Freiburg: Herder Verlag, 1982), 109, transl. Ellie Eich

CHAPTER 3: THE SUFI COLOR

1. Georg Schmid, *Die Mystik der Weltreligion, "Aus den Reden Buddhas", (Kreuz, Zurich, 1990),* 142, abbreviated; transl. Ellie Eich
2. Irina Tweedie, *Daughter of Fire,* (Blue Dolphin Publishing, 1986), 766

CHAPTER 4: THE PATH I

1. Rumi, *Sieh! Das ist Liebe,* (Basel: Sphinx Verlag, 1993), 51, transl. Ellie Eich

CHAPTER 5: THE PATH II

1. Irina Tweedie, Der Weg durchs Feuer, (Interlaken: Ansata Verlag), 237, transl. Ellie Eich
2. Sloterdijk/Buber, *Mystische Zeugnisse aller Zeiten und Voelker,* (Munich: Diederichs, 1993), 135, transl. Ellie Eich
3. Hafiz, *Liebesgeschichten,* (Frankfurt/Main: Insel 1984), 55, abbreviated; transl. Ellie Eich
4. Rumi, *Sieh! Das ist Liebe,* (Basel: Sphinx Verlag, 1993), 39, transl. Ellie Eich

5. Schimmel, *Mystische Dimensionen des Islam,* (Aalen: Qalandar 1979), 324, transl. Ellie Eich

6. Farid ud-Din Attar, *The Conference of the Birds,* (London: Penguin Books, 1984), 166

CHAPTER 7: THE TEACHER

1. Georg Schmid, *Die Mystik der Weltreligion, "Aus den Reden Buddhas", (Kreuz, Zurich, 1990),* 46, transl. Ellie Eich

Made in the USA
Lexington, KY
27 January 2017